Ben   Benton, Barbara
       Ellis Island

DATE DUE

ELLIS ISLAND

ELLIS ISLAND
A PICTORIAL HISTORY

Barbara Benton

Facts On File Publications
New York, New York ● Oxford, England

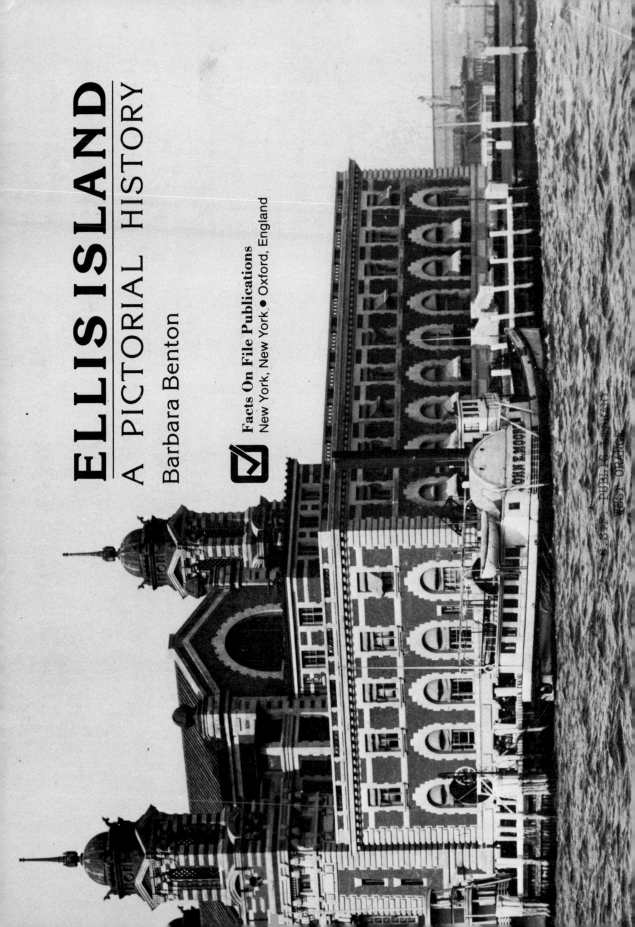

Design by Stephanie Schaffer

Contemporary photographs
principally by Julian Kaiser

Published by Facts On File, Inc.
460 Park Avenue South
New York, New York 10016

**Library of Congress Cataloging in
Publication Data**

Benton, Barbara.
  Ellis Island.
  Includes index.
  1. Ellis Island Immigration Station
—History.   2. Ellis Island Immigration Station—Conservation and restoration.   3. United States—Emigration
and immigration—History. I. Title.
JV6483.B47 1985
325'.1'0973
84-10154
ISBN 0-8160-1124-9

Type set in Korinna by Werner Graphics

Printed on 70-pound Glatco
by Maple Vail

Produced by Barbara Benton
2465 Palisade Avenue
Riverdale, New York 10463

First Edition

Printed in the United States of America

10 9 8 7 6 5 4 3 2

ACKNOWLEDGMENTS

Without the inspiration and encouragement of Julian Kaiser, I would not have begun this book. Without the empathy and support of Stephanie Schaffer, I might not have finished it. I am grateful to them both, not only for friendship, but for absolute professionalism under any and all conditions.

I would like to thank a number of other people, too, for invaluable assistance: Michael Adlerstein, Director of the National Park Service Statue of Liberty/Ellis Island Restoration Project, gave me his support early on, as well as access to NPS resource materials and to the restoration site. Architects John Stubbs, James Rhodes, and Frank Matero and historian Fred Wasserman of Beyer Blinder Belle shared textual and illustrative materials and hours of their time as I prepared the chapters on construction and restoration. Donald Porter, formerly of Notter Finegold Alexander, now of Philip Johnson/John Burgee, provided many factual details about the restoration and insights into the inner workings of so vast and complicated a design project. My colleagues at Rebus, Inc., especially Shirley Tomkievicz, shared their editorial experience and expertise: Mary Jenkins advised me on picture research; Michael Goldman copy-edited the manuscript. Kate Kelly, my mentor at Facts-on-File, made many intelligent editorial suggestions and was ever responsive to my "writerly" needs. My friends Ira Meistrich and Bonnie Quinn read the book in mechanical. Bob Brier and Elaine were there for Ian, as always, while I immersed myself in this project, which must have seemed never-ending. Thank you, all.

CONTENTS

The Statue of Liberty was assembled and copper-plated in 1883 outside the Paris studio of its creator, August Bartholdi. In dedicatory ceremonies on October 28, 1886, the statue was presented by the people of France to the people of the United States. Originally a symbol of liberty, in years to come the statue also became a more general symbol of welcome to the United States.

INTRODUCTION

Ellis Island is a 27½-acre piece of landfill in upper New York Bay, about one mile southwest of the tip of Manhattan. Compared to the total area of the United States, it is geographically insignificant. But to millions of people over a period of six decades, it was overwhelmingly important: It was their first experience of America, the gateway to a new land and a new life.

From 1892 to 1954 Ellis Island was the prime immigrant receiving station in the United States. Some 12 million people—of all nationalities, but mostly Eastern European Jews, Poles, Italians, Austrians, Hungarians, and Slovaks—were "processed" for entry on this tiny island. After sometimes weeks at sea, they at last arrived in New York harbor, within sight of the Statue of Liberty. They were then ferried from their ocean-going vessels to Ellis, where, exhausted, confused, and apprehensive, they were given a battery of legal and medical examinations by immigration inspectors before they were allowed to come into the country. Most got through in a few hours; about twenty percent were detained for further questioning and observation; two percent were deported. It was a pivotal experience, sometimes harrowing, always dramatic.

The facility at Ellis Island was an elaborate complex, with waiting rooms, dormitories, kitchens, dining halls, hospital wards, docks and wharves, a post office, a customs house, a money exchange, a railway ticketing office, a telegraph station, staff offices and residences, a greenhouse, even a mortuary. The Registry, or Great Hall, as it has come to be called, where most of the processing took place, was the most imposing room—in both size and significance—that many of the immigrants had ever been in.

But the island station, built to accommodate less than a quarter of a million immigrants a year, was woefully inadequate for the millions who flooded into this country from 1900 to 1915, the peak of the greatest mass movement in history. In 1907, the most active year, more than 1.2 million people passed through. (Ellis was only one of seventy receiving stations in the country at the time, but it handled ninety percent of all immigrants.) These people and their descendents now number perhaps 100 million, or about forty percent of the current population.

After 1914 the flood of immigrants began to subside, and after the 1920s, with the passing of the quota laws, it diminished to a trickle. The large facility was no longer necessary, and Ellis was, over the next thirty years, relegated to other uses, mainly as a detention center for deportees, a hospital for wounded servicemen, and a Coast Guard station. Finally, in 1954, declared "excess federal property," it was boarded up and abandoned. For the next two decades, it slowly weathered and ruined, prey to thieves and vandals. In 1965 it became part of the National Park Service, administered by the same office as the Statue of Liberty.

In 1982 the Reagan administration announced the formation of the Statue of Liberty/Ellis Island Centennial Commission. The purpose of the commission is to raise funds for the restoration of the two landmarks, to have the statue completed in time for its centennial celebration in 1986, and to advise the National Park Service and Department of the Interior on establishing a national monument to the immigrants.[1] "The Statue of Liberty and Ellis Island, together with the Castle Clinton National Monument on the Battery and the New Jersey Shoreline Park, are slated to be a historical-educational-recreational complex in New York harbor capable of serving more than 2 million visitors a year."

The restoration plan depends upon the suc-

cess of the commission in raising the estimated $230 million needed to restore the Statue of Liberty and Ellis Island. Public response has so far been gratifying. Millions have been contributed by individuals, corporations, foundations, unions, and ethnic and civic organizations.

Repairs on the statue are well underway, and by the 1986 centennial celebration she will be completely restored, with a new torch, new stainless-steel supports, a glass-walled hydraulic elevator, and improved facilities for visitors. On Ellis Island restoration work for now is centering on the main building, particularly the Registry, which is being restored to the 1918–1924 period. The work includes removal of walls and other structures installed after the main immigration period, repairs to the building, and restoration of historic areas. The goal is to have the Registry completed and Ellis Island open again to visitors by the summer of 1987. Then a master plan for the

In 1983, exactly a century after its completion in Paris, scaffolding again went up around the Statue of Liberty as French craftsmen worked to repair the beloved landmark in time for its centennial celebration in 1986.

BARBARA BENTON

restoration and development of the rest of the island will be put into effect. The entire project will be completed by 1992, the centennial of the opening of the Ellis Island immigration station and, incidentally, the fifth centennial of the discovery of America by Columbus and the beginning of immigration here.

This book is intended to give, in words and pictures, a history of Ellis Island from its opening in 1892 to its closing in 1954, including details of the current restoration effort. Because it is important to realize that the particular history of Ellis Island is part of the continuum of immigration since the origin of our country, the book begins with an overview of immigration before the opening of formal receiving stations and ends with a description of recent policy—the possible effects of pending legislation and prospects for the future. We are a nation of immigrants. We should not forget what it was—and is—like to come to America.

CHAPTER ONE

HISTORY

Immigration to America began with its discovery by European explorers and increased steadily, unchecked and unregulated, until the mid-nineteenth century, when Castle Garden, the predecessor of Ellis Island, became the first formal receiving station anywhere. In 1855 Samuel Waugh painted the new station (right) of Irish immigrants disembarking in New York. Although the vessel seen here is a sailing ship, which may have taken as long as two months to cross the Atlantic, steamships by then were making the trip in less than two weeks, contributing to the increase in arrivals.

MUSEUM OF THE CITY OF NEW YORK

Even the Indians, the only true "native" Americans, were also migrants. They came to the New World over a prehistoric land bridge from Asia, settled here, and developed for thousands of years before the first European explorers discovered them in the fifteenth century. They eased the white man's way into the continent, taught him how to survive in the wilderness, and ultimately were displaced by him.

The Spanish came first, then the Dutch, the Swedish, the English, the French, the Germans, and the Scotch-Irish. In addition, thousands of blacks were brought here as slaves. The English were the most numerous, bringing with them their language and other Anglo-Saxon traditions that largely became the basis of the American way of life.

Patterns of settlement were determined by the type and availability of land and employment, approximating conditions in settlers' homelands. The Spanish, in search of gold, explored and settled Florida, New Mexico, and southern California. The Dutch and English tended to stay on the Eastern Seaboard, where they capitalized on the bounty of the sea and engaged in foreign trade. The French explored the east, then struck out for the interior, trading with the Indians and settling in pockets both north and south. The Swedish and later the Norwegians went to the midwestern prairies and to the north-central timberlands, which closely resembled Scandinavia. The Germans, too, liked the Midwest, but also were drawn to the hills of Pennsylvania, as were the Scotch-Irish. Blacks were imported to the South, where they became the mainstay of an agrarian economy. In general, immigrants tended to avoid the South, where there was less opportunity for employment. The Scotch-Irish, an exception, settled in the deep southern backwoods—

as far away from Englishmen as they could get.

For the first 200 years of colonization, growth was slow and communities were small. In 1680 the population was about 200,000; in 1776 it still was only about 2 million. Yet, by Revolutionary times, when an immigrant stepped off the boat he no longer encountered the same hardships as the early settlers. He found small towns and some large cities, judicial and educational systems, churches and businesses, books and newspapers, comfortable homes, and enough of his native countrymen to feel kinship.

A new citizen of the world emerged, the American, and he was a blend of many nationalities. In *Letters from an American Farmer*, published in 1782, Michel-Guillaume Jean de Crevecoeur wrote that the American

. . . is either an European, or the descendant of an European, hence that strange mixture of blood, which you will find in no other country. I could point out to you a family whose grandfather was an Englishman, whose wife was Dutch, whose son married a French woman, and whose present four sons have now four wives of different nations. . . .

This cosmopolitan man was likely to be a strong personality, an adventurer of capital or talent who had been willing to take the risk of leaving home in search of freedom, fortune, or fame. He might have been a gentleman, a merchant, a banker, a farmer, a craftsman—or an indigent peasant. Very likely, during the early years of settlement, he was a refugee from religious oppression.

The religious turmoil of the sixteenth century had left Europe divided in factions, all intolerant of each other. Any religious minority unwilling to surrender its faith suffered persecution. Although religious liberty was not firmly established in the New World until near the end of the eighteenth century, nearly every sect sought and found safety somewhere in America.

The onset of the French Revolution in 1789 marked the beginning of nearly a century of governmental upheaval in Europe, so that in the late eighteenth and nineteenth centuries political refugees joined the religious immigrants in America.

Subtler, less direct forces—economic—also drove people out of Europe. After the middle of the seventeenth century, with the beginning of technological advancement, the quality of life improved. As the mortality rate declined, the population rose dramatically, increasing by more than 100 million every one hundred years. The existing economy simply could not support such numbers, and the surplus population was set in motion.

Something we now call the "Agricultural Revolution" was a factor in the economic upheaval. Since medieval times, farming had been a communal activity, with land divided in small plots among the peasants. Increasingly, farming was taken over by large landowners who used new methods and machinery to cultivate large crops. Many small farmers, even the relatively well-to-do, failed to compete, lost their farms, and went to the New World in search of new land.

The United States offered newcomers relatively easy land ownership. Land was cheap and abundant; the government was involved only in a limited way to make sure that its distribution was equitable. Through most of the eighteenth century, constant expansion toward the frontiers and the need to conquer the wilderness ensured that newcomers willing to work the land would be welcome.

Along with the Agricultural Revolution in Europe came the Industrial Revolution, which eventually replaced traditional handicrafts, another means by which the peasantry had made a living. Great factories using machinery and cheap unskilled labor turned out large quantities of goods at prices the traditional craftsman could not match. Displaced craftsmen were anxious to emigrate; the thriving economy in America beckoned.

As the economic situation for peasants in Europe worsened and the numbers of immigrants increased, more and more were unable to pay their own way here. A system of indentured servitude arose: In return for his passage, a man would contract with a sea captain to work for a period of years for whoever bought his contract. The sea captain earned a fee, the immigrant got his passage, and the person who bought the contract got a laborer. Later, more formal contracts for labor were instituted; but when industrial society in America became more complex, organized labor here strenuously objected to such practices.

During the American and French revolutionary wars, immigration was scant. Because travel across the Atlantic was unsafe, no more than 10,000 people a year came to America. With the end of the War of 1812 and the Napoleonic Wars, however, normal travel once again became possible. Postwar economic conditions in Europe were such that there was an even greater exodus than before. The years from 1820 to 1870 marked the first modern "wave of immigration." In all, nearly 7.4 million people entered America during this period —the rate slackening only during the Civil War. They came predominantly from Great Britain, Ireland, Scandinavia, and Germany, but also—for the first time —from the Orient. Over 100,000 Chinese settled on the West Coast to work on the railroads and in the mines. There were 112,000 known immigrants from Canada as well.

Changes in the economic organization profoundly affected the Jews of Europe, who had for centuries acted as intermediaries, trading between the peasants and people in the cities. The elimination of this role, together with religious discrimination, caused many Central and Eastern European Jews to begin to move westward. It was the beginning of the shift from the "old" immigrants—those from Western and Northern Europe—to the "new," including the Jews, Poles, Italians, Austrians, Hungarians, and Slavs.

In 1862 Congress passed the Homestead Act to encourage people to settle west of the Mississippi River. The act provided that a man could earn title to 160 acres simply by living on them and cultivating them for five years—so long as he was an American citizen or formally declared his intention to become one. It was the best land deal yet, precipitating a rush to the West.

A depression in the early 1870s limited immigration again for a short time, but with the first sign of recovery the numbers began to climb once more, creating a "second wave" as great as the first. More than ever before the causes were closely related to the effects of industrialization. In Europe factory production and scientific agriculture ruthlessly displaced more and more people, while in America a rapid industrial expansion generated more and more jobs for skilled and semiskilled laborers. The hours were long and the wages were low, but compared to conditions in Europe, America seemed rich in opportunity. Those who wanted to work could find jobs. Some of the earlier immigrants had opened small businesses of their own. Some had achieved wealth, or seen their children do so. These successes encouraged those still in Europe considering emigration in the belief that prosperity could be had in America, along with political and religious freedom.

It is difficult to assess all the factors that caused people to emigrate to America. Certainly it is useful to consider the general economic and socio-political influences, but one must remember that emigrants were individuals who had specific, personal reasons for wanting to leave their homes and travel great distances for an uncertain future in a faraway place. Local conditions (perhaps a drought, an epidemic, or a war) and personal circumstances (unemployment, a failed marriage, or fear of conscription) were the immediate precipitating factors.

The development of worldwide communications—a publishing industry and an expanded, reliable mail service—was also an influence. Never before had so much information been available. Many people could not read, but there was always someone in a community, usually a doctor, a teacher, or minister, who would read aloud to others, and a newspaper or letter might circulate from household to household for weeks, until the next communication arrived.

Travel books—reminiscences of personal experiences written by wealthy, educated travelers—were generally truthful sources of information, as were formal guidebooks, but these were not widely distributed among the poorer classes. More commonly read were newspaper and magazine articles, which tried to capitalize on the current interest in emigration. The information in these was of variable reliability.

More blatantly propagandistic were the pamphlets and posters published by real estate companies, railroads, and shipping lines. These were intended to sell land and travel arrangements and were in stiff competition with each other, so the material usually exaggerated the bountifulness of America.

Literature was issued, too, by immigration bureaus set up by population-hungry American states—Ver-

Illustrated newspapers reflected the 1860s rush to the West. Here, immigrants line up to apply for naturalization so that they can be eligible for land under the provisions of the Homestead Act.

Because they had vast acreages of land to sell, American railroad companies vigorously promoted the settlement of the West. The Union Pacific alone claimed to have advertised in 2,000 American and European newspapers.

mont, Georgia, Michigan, Missouri, and California, to name a few. The Wisconsin bureau, for instance, published pamphlets in seven languages and advertised in foreign journals. The back page of the Colorado pamphlet, published in 1872 and entitled *Colorado, a Statement of Facts*, is representative of the propaganda:

Those who are restless in their old homes, or who seek to better their condition, will find greater advantages in Colorado than anywhere else in the West. Our mining resources offer inducements which no state east of the mountains can present, and for stockmen and agriculturalists Colorado can make a better exhibit than any other region. The climate possesses peculiar charms and those in failing health, or invalids can find here a sure panacea for nearly every human ill. The poor should come to Colorado, because here they can by industry and frugality better their condition. The rich should come here, because they can more advantageously invest their means than in any other region. The young should come here to get an early start on the road to wealth, and the old should come to get a new lease on life, and to enjoy their declining years in a country unequalled for its natural beauty and loveliness. In short, it is the Mecca for all classes and all conditions, and we confidently recommend it to the thoughtful examination of the public.

It is impossible to calculate the effects of such advertisements. Certainly the midwestern states attracted a huge number of immigrants, but it must be noted that the native-born population increased at a similar rate.

Probably much more persuasive than anything in the barrage of printed matter were letters from friends and relatives who had already emigrated. These letters, coming from known individuals and containing local details in familiar language, must have been more credible than advertising. Most of those that survive were printed in newspapers, presumably because editors believed they would be of interest to readers, and so they are, to some degree, selected, but they provide some evidence of the type of letters that came from America. Most reassured that life in America was indeed materially better than in Europe. "We now have a comfortable dwelling and two acres of ground planted with potatoes, Indian corn, melons, etc. I have two hogs, one ewe and a lamb: cows in the spring were as high as 33 dollars, but no doubt I shall have one in the fall." Or, "A breakfast here consists of chicken, mutton, beef, or pork, warm or cold wheat bread, butter, white cheese, eggs, or small pancakes, the best coffee, tea, cream, and sugar . . . and my greatest regret here is to see the superabundance of food, much of which has to be thrown to the chickens and the swine." "I am living in God's noble and free soil, neither am I a slave under others . . . I have now been on American soil two and a half years, and I have not been compelled to pay a penny for the privilege of living. Neither is my cap worn out from lifting it in the presence of gentlemen." (Excerpts are from *The Distant Magnet* by Philip Taylor.)

Frequently, one who had emigrated would return home—sometimes to stay, but more often temporarily—to pay respects, prove his affluence, deliver goods or money, or escort other family members to America. Such a visitor was treated with the utmost respect, and people from miles around would go to him to ask questions and hear tales of his adventures. An uncalculated number of emigrants went to America seasonally just to work, then would return home to spend winters with their families. These "birds of passage" did much to

A White Star Line advertisement, printed by an Irish agency in the 1880s, pictures an early-model steamship which, although it has two stacks, also features sails like the old clipper ships.

Emigrants in Warsaw apply for passports to America. After 1882, steamship companies were responsible for a preliminary screening of passengers and were financially liable for inadmissible persons they transported to the United States. Eventually the largest lines established elaborate emigrant villages in European ports to facilitate the screening.

spread the word about America (and to confuse American immigration statistics—indications are that only sixty-seven percent of all "immigrants" stayed in America).

In communities all over Europe, emigration was a prime topic of conversation. There was hardly anyone anywhere who did not know of someone who had gone to America and prospered. The American consul in Naples reported in 1890 that the most frequent reply to the question "Why are you emigrating?" was "My friend in America is doing well and he has sent for me."

Of course, it is naive to assume that literally everyone wanted to go to America. Although the majority of the millions who emigrated from Europe between 1880 and 1921 went to the United States, many others were not struck with "America fever." The causes and currents of emigration were manifold, and the records are inexact, but for every person who came, there were many who moved elsewhere—to Brazil, Argentina, Australia, and Canada, for example—or who simply moved to a neighboring country, nearby town, or adjacent community. And there were many more who stayed where they were.

Once the decision had been made to emigrate, however, technological advancements in travel after the 1840s made it easier than ever to go—and to return, if one wished. Previously, the trek overland to the port of embarkation had been arduous enough: Many hiked for hundreds of miles with their belongings on their backs or in carts, which, if they could not afford a draft animal, they pushed or pulled themselves. Some were able to travel part of the way by riverboat. Always, progress was slow, taking as long as a year. Religious or political fugitives, especially Jews, had to take great care at the border crossings in order not to be apprehended by authorities. All emigrants were

vulnerable to thieves and extortionists. Tickets and passports (and later, medical certificates) sometimes were available only at the right price, and at almost every stopping there was some additional fee to pay. The trip overland—with all its difficulties, delays, and expenses—depleted emigrants' resources to the point that many were desperate with anxiety by the time they made ship. But by the end of the nineteenth century, millions of miles of European railway tracks made the journey to port less exhausting and dangerous, and in some countries it was possible to buy a through ticket to final destination.

Once in port—in the days of sailing ships, this was usually Liverpool—an emigrant had to choose among a confusing array of shipping lines and accommodations. Trying to avoid thieves, prostitutes, and runners with various services to sell, an emigrant walked the docks and, with an unpracticed eye, attempted to judge the quality of the ships he had to choose among. When his selection was made, he struck a bargain with the captain or an agent. Until 1850 there was no government regulation of this sort of negotiation—or of conditions aboard ship.

By the early nineteenth century, cheap passage was made possible by the booming export of grain, cotton, and timber from the United States and Canada to Europe. Lightly laden, westbound ships would fill their holds with steerage passengers on the return trip. The fare from Liverpool to New York, for instance, dropped from twelve pounds in 1816 to just over three in 1846.

Sailing ships were designed for carrying cargo, not passengers, and there was little effort to adapt them for human comfort. Apart from bringing on provisions (flour, potatoes, oatmeal, tea, some salted fish) and water (often stored in rancid casks previously used for oil or other contaminants), a captain merely would lay

An engraving in the April 9, 1870, issue of Harper's Weekly ran with the following copy: STEERAGE BUNKS. The discomforts of a long ocean voyage are sufficiently trying to the nerves, even when alleviated by all the luxuries and comforts of the first-cabin. To be sure, the first-cabin, or saloon, as it is now generally called, is small and cramped, and the state-rooms are narrow, dark, and close; but these accommodations are palatial in comparison with the steerage—the quarters where the poor emigrants are huddled together like beasts in pens. Their Atlantic voyage is any thing but a holiday trip. They are literally packed together in a dark, cavernous part of the vessel; they have but little space among the ropes and beams of the forward decks wherein to "take the air"; and they must live during the voyage in an atmosphere which is close at best, and is too often tainted with disease. See, in the picture, how they are crowded up together, and how rude are their berths and surroundings! The poor ill woman in the corner has scarcely space to move; one man's berth is so narrow that his feet project over it. Still, the emigrants make the best of things. Some one has given the shaggy-haired little girl a toy, which she exultingly displays to her sea-sick mother; another little girl is unraveling a string puzzle; and the interested faces of the two women who are watching her show that even in this dark hole there are cheerful, contented souls. On calm nights, when the sea is still, and the steamer rolls steadily and gently across the waves, you may hear songs rising from the steerage, and see the emigrants standing in groups on the forward deck, the men smoking and chewing, and the women, their arms burdened with infants, chatting together and watching the spray and the surging sea.

BARBARA BENTON

down a temporary deck over the cargo area and construct narrow, flimsy berths that could be dismantled after the voyage.

Passengers were packed tightly, often with no more than a few square feet of space per person. There were no latrines and no windows, so sanitation and ventilation were serious problems. Conditions varied among vessels, but nearly all emigrants on sailing ships, regardless of class, had to suffer overcrowding and disorder, seasickness, a foul atmosphere, and poor food. A trip took anywhere from five weeks to two months; a few recorded trips took 100 days or more. A storm could make things much worse. With the ship pitching and creaking, decks awash, hatches battened down, people sick everywhere, it was a miserable experience.

Worse yet was the knowledge that at any moment disaster could strike in the form of fire, shipwreck, or epidemic. On a wooden ship lighted candles and open cooking fires were a constant hazard. It was not unusual for more than 100 people to die of shipboard fires in a single year. Shipwrecks, too, took their toll. In the terrible winter of 1853-54, 200 German immigrants drowned when their ship was driven onto the New Jersey shore, and 480 emigrants and their ship out of Glasgow disappeared altogether.

Much more common—and lethal—were epidemics. Typhus, or "ship fever," spread by lice, produced a frightful mortality rate. In 1847, the worst year of the Irish famine, a total of 7,000 emigrants died of typhus at sea and 10,000 more after arrival in Quebec. Another deadly scourge was Asiatic cholera, caused by an intestinal microbe and spread in contaminated water. The worst year for cholera was 1853, when ten to fifteen percent of the passengers on some ships succumbed to the disease.

With all the dire possibilities, there still were pleasant moments at sea. Certainly, no entertainment was provided by the shipping lines, but in good weather, passengers could go on deck. Men and boys might help the sailors haul sail or make repairs. Women and girls sat on deck reading or chatting. Children played with homemade toys, marbles, cards, and dominoes. There were worship services, sometimes music and dancing.

With the advent of steam, the quality of the transatlantic passage was gradually elevated from potentially deadly to merely uncomfortable. By the 1870s the trip had been shortened to ten to fourteen days on the average, reducing the threat of epidemics. Typhus and smallpox still cropped up occasionally, but at least all ships by then had physicians on staff, and conditions in steerage had been improved enough to control contagion to some degree. Ships were made of iron, so they were less vulnerable to fire and shipwreck, although when one did occur the result could be disastrous. As a result of investigations, mainly by the United States and Great Britain, shipping lines were required to provide better services and accommodations. Passengers were still required to bring their bedding and most of what they needed to prepare food, but the ships did supply better-quality provisions than previously and galleys stocked with ranges, boilers, and vegetable cookers. Most immigrants continued to bring food with them, but extra could be bought, albeit exorbitantly, from the crews. Some of the better shipping lines provided cooked meals three times a day. Toilet facilities varied. Ventilation remained poor.

News that land was in sight always excited the weary passengers, who did the best they could to clean up and organize themselves for arrival. If they came into New York harbor by night, the thrill had to be postponed until morning; but by day, crowding out on

Rare photographs of steerage passengers relaxing on deck were produced in the 1890s and early 1900s by the popular stereo-view camera. The double images, or "stereos," (halves of which are seen here), collected then as now by armchair travelers, are given a three-dimensional effect when viewed through a special apparatus.

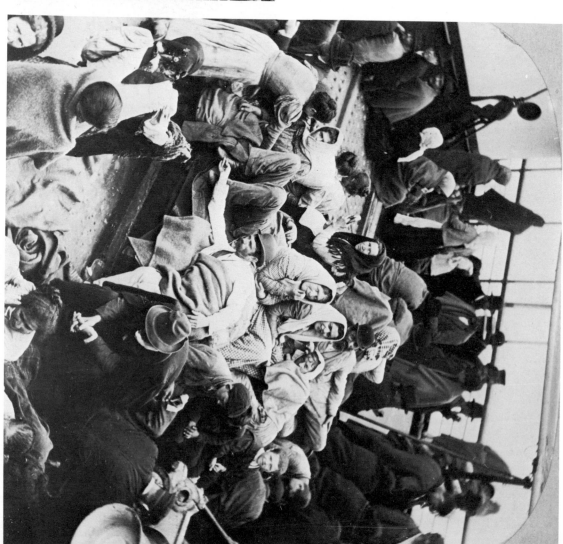

A staff artist for Leslie's Illustrated Newspaper sketched immigrants on the steerage deck of a steamer entering New York harbor in 1887. Few of the immigrants would have known what the newly erected Statue of Liberty symbolized.

deck, the joyous and apprehensive immigrants could see many other big ships, some also with crowded decks, and the tall buildings of New York City. After 1886 the most impressive structure in sight was the 300-foot, copper-clad Statue of Liberty, a gift from the French to the American people. Although the statue had been highly publicized for ten years prior to its actual dedication, and in years to come would be a world-famous symbol of welcome, many of the immigrants were vague about what it was. One popular misconception was that it was the tomb of Christopher Columbus.

Landing was always chaotic. Before 1847 boarding-house runners, tavern keepers, and peddlers were allowed on board to make bargains directly with the confused newcomers. Once on the dock it was worse, with no interference from the police. Immigrants might be cheated while exchanging money, sold tickets to wrong destinations at inflated prices, bilked by all manner of merchants, and enticed to flea-bitten boarding houses, where they were further taken advantage of. Young women were tempted into moral danger. Private welfare agencies offered some protection, but it was only after the creation of the New York State Immigration Commission that there was any regulation of landing procedures and licensing of concessionaires. In 1855 the commission created the first formal receiving station anywhere in the world—Castle Garden. Originally Fort Clinton, it was for over 100 years part of the Battery defense system. In 1822 it was ceded to New York City by the federal government, renamed, and converted to a "resort" and concert hall. The famous soprano Jenny Lind performed there for a packed house.

For thirty-five years Castle Garden operated as the receiving station in New York, where by the end of the nineteenth century seventy-five percent of all immigrants to the United States landed. Accounts from the 1860s and early 1870s describe the procedure: After medical inspection at Staten Island, where, if necessary, quarantines were administered, ships docked at either Hudson or East River piers. Immigrants went quickly through customs, after which first- and second-class passengers were discharged. Steerage passengers then went by barge to Castle Garden, where they were "registered"—a process that included little more than recording names. There they could change money, buy rail tickets, receive any communications or visitors that might await them, send letters or telegrams, deposit valuables for a short time, and meet with representatives of various welfare organizations. Runners were excluded, translators in several languages were available, and an employment agency just outside Castle Garden helped at least some immigrants to find work immediately. Eventually, a hospital for minor illnesses was added to the depot; serious cases were sent to Ward's Island. There was a restaurant, run under contract, where beer could be bought for ten cents a bottle, coffee for five cents a cup, and large sandwiches for thirteen cents. While it was true that some officials were guilty of taking advantage of immigrants, and waterfront sharpies were ever ready to pounce just outside the gate, the worst forms of abuse had been eliminated. After the opening of Castle Garden, it was at least possible for an immigrant to land in New York without molestation.

Once out of Castle Garden, however, immigrants' reception in New York was anything but warm. Residents and merchants in the vicinity of the docks were disgusted by the bedlam and insistent that stricter regulations be imposed. The first welfare system in the world was established in New York, not as the result of

Castle Garden, which preceded Ellis Island as the immigrant receiving station in New York, was a product of the tensions of the Napoleonic era. Originally a "battery," or fortress, it was intended, along with four other forts in or on the harbor, to defend New York from the British. After the War of 1812, it was named Castle (or Fort) Clinton in honor of DeWitt Clinton, a former mayor of New York City and governor of New York State. Abandoned by the military in 1822, it was renamed Castle Garden and leased by New York City as a place of public entertainment. In the 1840s it was roofed over and used for operatic concerts. The 1845 season opened with Semiramide and The Barber of Seville. One critic wrote that the audience was "regaled with the choicest Italian music and the most inspiring mint juleps." In 1850 P.T. Barnum presented the "Swedish Nightingale," Jenny Lind, in her American debut. The watercolor at right was painted in 1854 by Albertus Van Beest, just one year before the first immigrants entered Castle Garden.

By the 1880s New York newspapers were reacting to the growing public concern about the "rising tide" of immigration. Harper's Weekly and Leslie's Illustrated were nevertheless liberal in attitude toward the hapless immigrant. The writer of the Harper's article illustrated by the engraving at far left said, "To reckon the value of immigration accurately . . . we must take into the account what it adds to our wealth in the establishment of new industries, and the strengthening of industries not new. By importing the artisans of Europe we import the arts of Europe, domesticate them, and find in them sources of enduring prosperity. . . ." Not everyone was so broad-minded about the impact of aliens on the labor force.

FRANK LESLIE'S
ILLUSTRATED
NEWSPAPER

No. 1313.—Vol. LI.   NEW YORK, NOVEMBER 27, 1880.   [Price 10 Cents.

BARBARA BENTON

BARBARA BENTON

a particularly liberal point of view, but out of dire need. By the end of the nineteenth century, New York State was spending $20 million annually for the care of paupers and the insane.

Immigrants were at best tolerated by New Yorkers—as by citizens elsewhere in the country—and at worst treated with savage contempt. Sometimes they were the victims of discrimination and even violence. They became the scapegoats for many societal evils—crime, urban slums, political corruption. Worse, as an unorganized faction of the labor force, they were held to be a threat to the national economy. They were the focal point of an entire political party, the "Know-Nothings," who organized to limit immigration to this country and to make citizenship difficult to attain.

But the immigrants' social welfare once on America's shores was not the only problem facing United States officials. The sheer number of hopeful newcomers arriving by the thousands each day was posing an administrative nightmare at Castle Garden and other receiving stations.

As a battlement, Castle Garden had stood 200 feet from shore in thirty-five feet of water, a drawbridge connecting it to the mainland. To adapt it to the reception of immigrants, the city of New York joined Castle Garden to the mainland by landfill and fenced it off from the immediate area. The illustrations here convey something of the atmosphere inside. Even today, without actually remembering why, an elderly person in New York might refer to a crowded, noisy place as "a regular Castle Garden."

NATIONAL PARK SERVICE

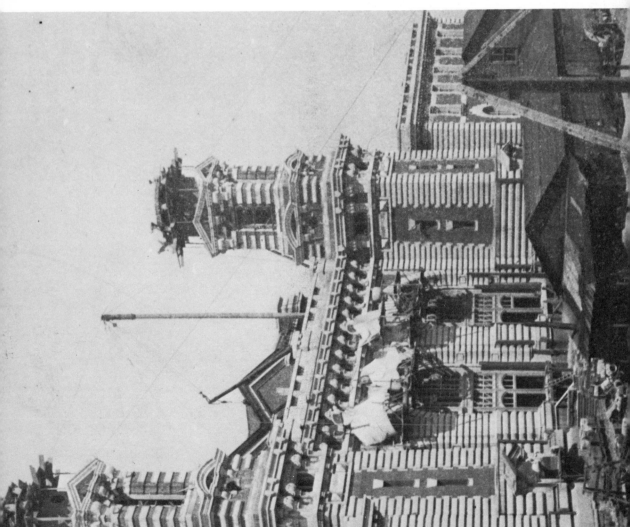

CHAPTER TWO
CONSTRUCTION

Construction of the buildings on Ellis Island, begun in 1890, took nearly ten years to complete. The first station burned in 1897, and although work on the second began within the same year, it was 1900 before the main building (left) was ready for use. Built of fireproof materials according to plans (detail, right) drawn by the architectural firm of Boring and Tilton, the new station was considered by architects, government officials, and the press to be more than adequate to handle the then declining numbers of immigrants.

By the 1870s the influx of foreign-born into the American labor market had reached a critical stage. Nationwide, workers were discomforted by the impact of the foreign competition on wages and working conditions. Several states attempted to pass laws limiting immigration, but these were declared unconstitutional on the grounds that they were illegal restrictions of interstate commerce. The problems, however, were so widespread and public reaction so vehement that the need for federal intervention was clear.

The first attempt by Congress to curb immigration was in response to a steadily increasing population of Chinese workers in California, where the foreign-born were roughly twenty-five percent of the total population. Public resentment was regularly expressed in the form of raids on Chinese neighborhoods. The California legislature had enacted laws that taxed only Chinese miners and fishermen, excluded the Chinese from hospitals and schools, banned their testimony in court, and prevented them from becoming citizens. Many of these laws were later declared unconstitutional, but public opinion at the time was unmistakable. In 1876 the California legislature investigated Chinese immigration and published a 300-page "report," well summarized by the following excerpt:

> During their entire settlement in California they have never adapted themselves to our habits, mode of dress, or our educational system, have never learned the sanctity of an oath, never desired to become citizens, or to perform the duties of citizenship, never discovered the difference between right and wrong, never ceased the worship of their idol gods, or advanced a step beyond the traditions of their native hive. Impregnable to all the influences of our Anglo-Saxon life, they remain the same stolid Asiatics that have floated on the rivers and slaved in the fields of China for thirty centuries of time.

In response to the crisis situation in California and aware of lesser problems nationwide, Congress in 1875 enacted the first restrictions against Orientals. This first act prohibited the transportation of Chinese and Japanese to the United States without their "free consent" or for "lewd or immoral" purposes. Incoming vessels were inspected for violations and their owners heavily penalized for transporting convicts and prostitutes.

This law was followed in 1882 by an even more stringently restrictionist act known as the Chinese Exclusion Act, which stopped all Chinese immigration for ten years and upheld the California law prohibiting citizenship. This policy toward the Chinese—expanded, defined, and refined over the years—continued until 1952, when the McCarran-Walter Act repealed all immigration and nationality laws extant and eliminated race as a barrier to immigration and naturalization.

Also in 1882, Congress enacted the first generally exclusive immigration law, which banned as an immigrant "any convict, lunatic, idiot, or any person unable to take care of himself or herself without becoming a public charge" and "all foreign convicts except those convicted of political offenses." If during examination at an immigration station a person was found to be any of the above, he was sent back to his nation of origin at the expense of the shipowner who transported him here.

In addition, this act established a fifty-cent head tax on any immigrant who entered the country by water.

The tax was used to defray the expenses of examination and to assist immigrants in need. The responsibility for the administration of the act was given to the Secretary of the Treasury. Local administration still was carried out by local officials appointed by governors.

Three years later, under pressure from organized labor, Congress passed the first of several alien contract labor laws. Basically, the laws, which were intended to aid the American working class, made it illegal for industrialists to import alien laborers—or to assist in their importation—in return for work or service of any kind. Certain kinds of immigrants were exempt from this ruling: foreigners and their employees temporarily living in the United States; skilled workmen for any new industry not established here; and professional performing artists and their relatives and personal friends already here. These laws, too, were administered by the Secretary of the Treasury, who assigned federal contract labor inspectors to Castle Garden.

A cooperative state and federal administration at Castle Garden continued until 1887, when an attack on the management of the receiving station led by the New York *World* precipitated an investigation of abuses. A committee appointed by the Secretary conducted a series of public hearings into charges that officials at Castle Garden failed to enforce immigration laws, particularly contract labor laws, and that they themselves took advantage of the immigrants. The investigative committee, concluding that the local administration at Castle Garden was a "perfect farce," recommended that the responsibility of immigration regulation be assumed by the federal government entirely.

Political cartoons reflected the anti-immigration sentiment of the times. President Benjamin Harrison—who later signed the resolution to remove the old powder magazine and convert Ellis Island into an immigration station—is seen here listening to Uncle Sam's opinion on where to draw the line on immigration.

Early in 1890 Secretary of the Treasury William Windom ended New York State involvement with immigration by revoking all contracts with local officials. (Contracts with authorities at Portland [Me.], Boston, Philadelphia, Baltimore, Key West, New Orleans, Galveston, and San Francisco remained in effect for another year.) Next he announced a decision to build a new receiving station on one of the federally owned islands in the New York harbor. His first choice was Bedloe's Island, but the press and public objected to such a "desecration" of the site of the newly erected Statue of Liberty. At that time a movement to remove a powder magazine from Ellis Island called attention to that island as a possible site for a new station.

Originally known as Gull Island, the three watery acres originally were bought by the Dutch from the Indians in 1630. Over a period of nearly two centuries it was called by several names: Oyster Island, from the oyster beds still numerous in the vicinity; Dyre's Island, after one of its owners; Bucking Island at the time of its inclusion in the New York City boundaries in 1730; then Gibbet or Anderson Island after the hanging of a pirate there in 1765 (there were other hangings as well). Near the end of the eighteenth century, the title to the island was acquired by a butcher named Samuel Ellis, who deeded it to his heirs; although it changed hands a few more times, the island kept his name.

In 1794 the War Department—because of threats of war first with Great Britain and later with France—decided to use the island as part of its defense of New York harbor, along with Bedloe's and Governor's islands. Title was bought from its owners for $10,000 by Governor Daniel Tompkins of New York, who then deeded it to the federal government.

Twice while buildings were under construction on Ellis Island—from 1890 to 1892 and from 1897 to 1900—the Barge Office served as an interim immigration station. In all, over a million immigrants were processed there.

The Army Chief of Engineers at first had in mind to build a castle there like the one on Governor's Island, but Ellis was too small and its foundations too soft for such a structure. So at first there was only a small casemated battery. By the outbreak of the War of 1812, there were twenty guns on the island, a magazine, and a small garrison. The little outpost actually saw no military action during the war—some British prisoners were held there briefly—and only afterwards was named Fort Gibson after a hero killed elsewhere.

In peacetime it was again used as a place for executing pirates, briefly as a recruit depot, and finally as a powder magazine, which it remained until 1890. From time to time, nearby New Jersey residents—or New York newspaper reporters in need of interesting copy—would sound alarm at the idea of powerful explosives sitting out in the harbor and agitate to have them removed. Publicity from one such outcry brought the attention of Secretary Windom to Ellis Island as a possible place for the new immigrant receiving station.

Of the three islands—Ellis, Bedloe's, and Governor's—Ellis was the least attractive, but it was the only one without powerful opposition to its being used for the immigration station. Consequently, in April 1890 the powder magazine was removed to Fort Wadsworth on the Narrows, and in May Congress appropriated $75,000 for the improvement of the island. In July workmen began dredging a channel for better access. Next they built crib works for landfill to increase the size of the island, docks, and pilings. Construction of the actual buildings, designed by the Office of the Superintendent of Repairs of U.S. Public Buildings in New York, took a year and half, in the course of which Congress appropriated additional funds for building.

In the meantime Castle Garden was closed down and immigrant processing was moved a short distance up the Battery to the Barge Office. Originally used by the Customs Bureau for inspection of first- and second-class passengers, the Barge Office was a cramped space, hardly adequate for the processing of large numbers of steerage passengers. Nevertheless, nearly 525,000 immigrants, eighty percent of the national total, passed through the Barge Office in the two-year interval between the closing of Castle Garden and the opening of Ellis Island. (Many of the employees at the Barge Office had been at Castle Garden, and some went on to work at Ellis Island as well.)

During the construction period Congress passed a law formally creating the Bureau of Immigration under the Department of the Treasury. Colonel John Weber was appointed the first Commissioner of Immigration.

When it opened in early January 1892, the new immigrant receiving station at Ellis Island consisted of twelve buildings, including a large two-story main processing building, built of pine and galvanized iron, a separate group of four hospital buildings, surgeon's quarters, record storage office, restaurant and kitchen building, detention building, disinfection house, boiler house, and tank and coal house. Total area of the island had been increased to about fourteen acres. Water was supplied by artesian wells and stored in cisterns. In addition, two ferry racks—one at Ellis and one at the Barge Office—had been built. The cost of the construction was about $500,000, nearly double the original estimate.

In an article entitled "Landing the Immigrants," which appeared in the October 24, 1891, issue of *Harper's Weekly,* writer Julian Ralph enthusiastically described the main building:

For a long time the great new building has been one of the sights for those who enjoy the Battery Park and those who cross the North River on the ferry-boats. It looks like a latter-day watering place hotel, presenting to the view a great many-windowed expanse of buff-painted wooden walls, of blue-slate roofing, and of light and picturesque towers. It is 400 feet long, two stories high, and 150 feet wide.... It is devised to permit the handling of at least 10,000 immigrants in a day, and the

first story, which is 13 feet in height, is sufficiently capacious for the storage and handling of the baggage of 12,000 newcomers....

Steerage passengers [will] ascend to the second-story for medical inspection and interrogation. Some [will] be detained for further physical examination; the others will continue on and into the great second-story room, to be separated into ten lines and to march through that number of aisles between the desks of the socalled 'pedigree clerks,' who will cross-examine them as the law requires. Beyond the aisles and the desks of the questioning inspectors they will find two great pens or enclosures.... Into one will go

The original main building—a tinderbox containing 4 million board feet of lumber—burned to the ground in less than three hours. No lives were lost, but all immigration records from Castle Garden were destroyed.

those whose destination is New York City or its suburbs; into the other will be put the greater number who are about to begin another journey to distant States and Territories.

On this second floor, conveniently arranged, are spaces for the railroad ticket-sellers, the clerks of the information bureau, for the telegraph and brokers' counters, and the lunch stand. Colonel John B. Weber, the commissioner of Emigration [sic] will have his office in one corner on that floor, and General O'Beirne, the Assistant Commissioner, will occupy a similar office in another corner. Accounts like the one above and a few drawings and

photographs are all that remain of the original station at Ellis Island. It had operated less than five years—processing nearly 1,644,000 immigrants— when shortly after midnight on June 14, 1897, it burned completely to the ground in less than three hours. Everyone on the island at the time—about 200 detained aliens and staff members—was safely evacuated, but all immigration records from 1855 to 1897, which had only that year been transferred to a vault on the island, were burned. Ironically, the final stage of improvements to the island—telephone and telegraph cables to New York City—had been completed only two days before.

With great relief that no lives were lost, Commissioner Joseph Senner and other officials immediately

The new main building, barely begun in the photo at right, was ornamented by four 100-foot towers. The copper-capped domes contained observatories commanding splendid views of the harbor and skyline.

NATIONAL ARCHIVES

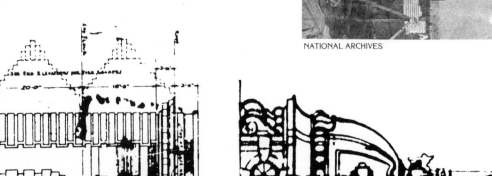

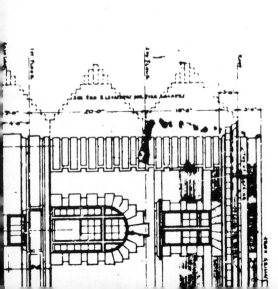

went to work to reconstruct the buildings, this time of fireproof materials. The Treasury Department estimated this would cost about $1.2 million, including enlargement of the island by another three acres and the construction of three brick and steel buildings—a main building, a hospital, and a restaurant.

Under the provisions of the Tarnsey Act of 1893, which for the first time allowed the department to solicit architectural designs and competitive bids on federal buildings from privately owned firms, five firms were asked to submit plans for the main building. A panel of another five architects was asked to serve as judges for the competition. (The main building at Ellis Island and the Post Office at Norfolk, Virginia, were the first federal buildings constructed under the provisions of the act, which has been in effect since then.)

In December 1897 the panel unanimously approved the plan submitted by the firm of Boring and Tilton. The design, comparatively economical, was predominantly of the French Renaissance style.

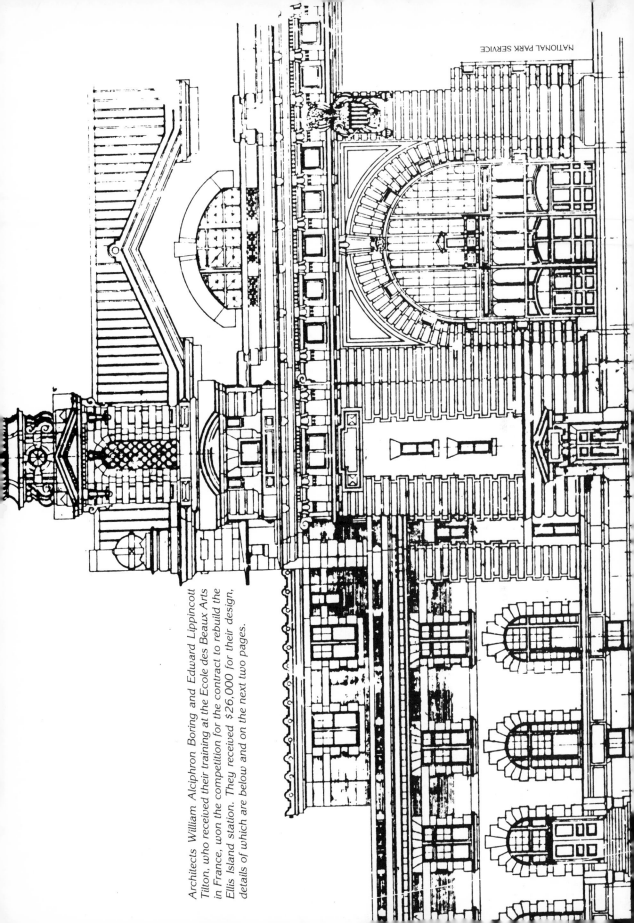

Architects William Alciphron Boring and Edward Lippincott Tilton, who received their training at the Ecole des Beaux Arts in France, won the competition for the contract to rebuild the Ellis Island station. They received $26,000 for their design, details of which are below and on the next two pages.

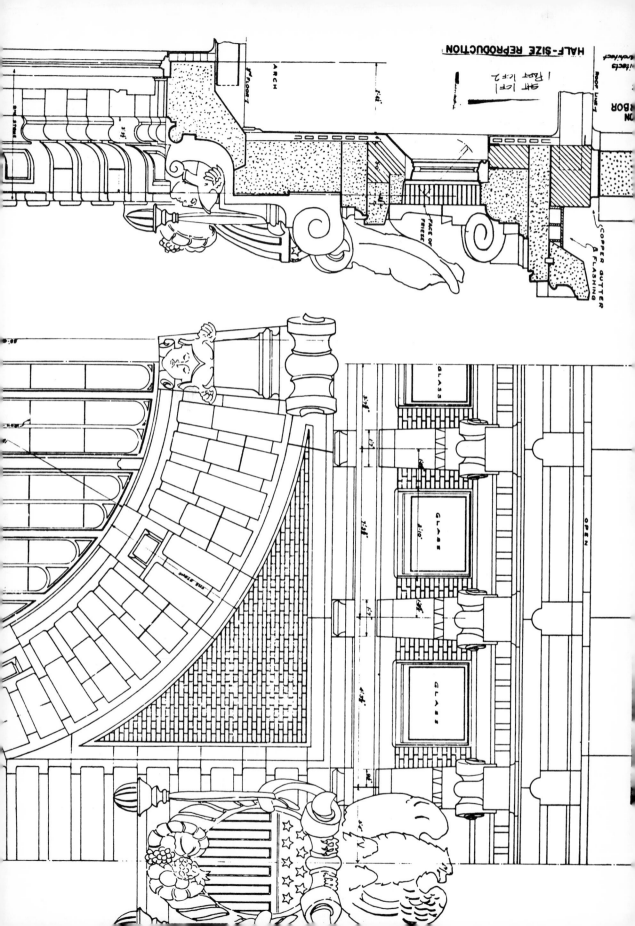

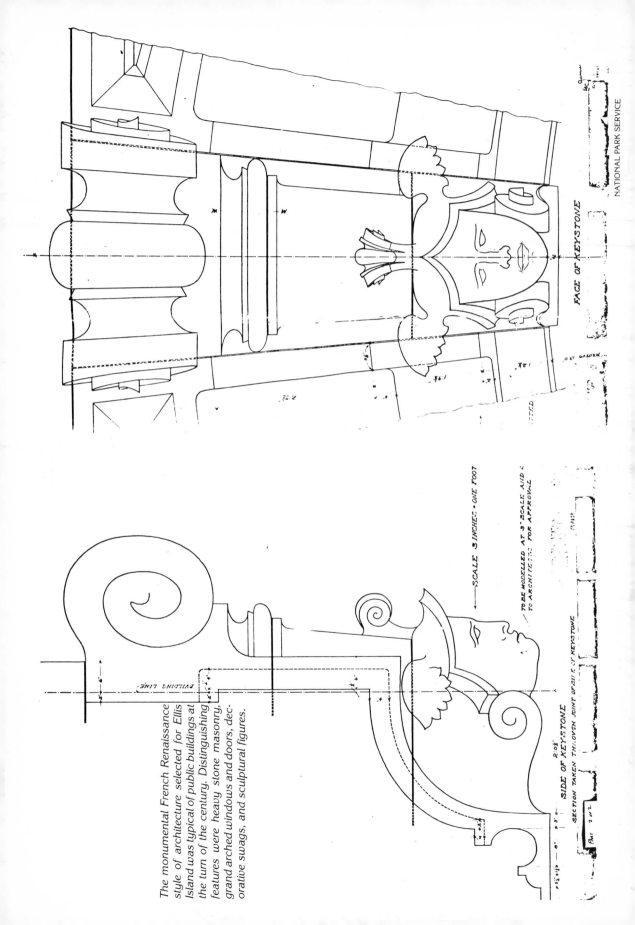

The monumental French Renaissance style of architecture selected for Ellis Island was typical of public buildings at the turn of the century. Distinguishing features were heavy stone masonry, grand arched windows and doors, decorative swags, and sculptural figures.

BUILDING LINE

SIDE OF KEYSTONE

SECTION TAKEN THROUGH JOINT OF SIDE OF KEYSTONE

FACE OF KEYSTONE

SCALE 3 INCHES = ONE FOOT

TO BE MODELLED AT 3" SCALE AND
TO ARCHITECTS FOR APPROVAL

Fireproof materials selected for the new buildings were red brick, held with Flemish bond, and generous trim of Indiana limestone and Maine granite (photo right). Many of the workmen (at right and on opposite page) were recent immigrants themselves. Italians, most notably, hired themselves out as bricklayers and stone masons, but many nationalities were represented among the Ellis Island construction crews.

NATIONAL ARCHIVES

Work proceeded slowly, beginning with the enlargement of the island and removal of debris from the fire. Meanwhile Boring and Tilton completed details of their design, which received considerable favorable publicity. An article in the February 26, 1898, issue of *Harper's Weekly* praised their plan, which provided a lot of greenery on the island and structures that would not only impress newcomers but would keep them free from outside interference until they were discharged, and at the same time would provide means for relatives and friends to communicate with them at the proper time. The article said the station would have

immense waiting rooms, men's and women's dormitories accommodating a possible total of fifteen hundred sleepers, a restaurant capable of supplying food to thousands, a hospi-

tal equipped for the treatment of any disease or emergency, docks and wharves with immediate transportation facilities for passengers and baggage to all points on this continent, a special post-office, custom-house, and telegraph station, with numberless administration offices, courts of inquiry, witness-rooms, detention pens, quarters for physicians, missionaries, employment and information bureaus, and sundry charitable enterprises, besides baths, lavatories, laundries, and abundant toilet facilities, and all the other needs of this greatest of caravanseries perched on an island of diminutive size.

While all this was under construction, the Barge Office was again put into use as a receiving station. Dr. Senner stepped down as Commissioner of Immigra-

Hospital buildings (photos opposite and below) were on Island 2, across from the main building. Built in a plain, functional style, they consisted of a surgeon's house, a forty-five-bed main building with a sixty-bed additional wing, and an outbuilding containing storeroom, laundry, morgue, and autopsy room. Later, island 3 was filled in and the Contagious Disease Hospital built.

tion, to be replaced by Thomas Fitchie, an appointee of President Grover Cleveland. Chronic management difficulties were passed from one administration to the next, particularly the impossibility of processing the volume of immigrants within the limited time and space and of protecting them from waterfront sharpies, some of whom were members of the immigration staff itself. There were simply too many opportunities for corruption. In 1899 a serious scandal and an investigation resulted in the dismissal of a number of employees, mostly of subordinate grades. But there was no thorough resolution.

The passage of national restrictive legislation, along with the assumption of federal control of immigration, had the effect of reducing the number of aliens coming to the United States from 1890 to 1900, but there were two other factors as well: a nationwide depression and a cholera scare. Presumably, word of economic hardship in the United States spread to foreign countries and discouraged the poor from migrating at that time. Certainly, the fear of an outbreak of cholera precipitated twenty-day quarantine restrictions on incoming vessels, discouraging them from leaving their ports of origin. Whatever the causes, the number of immigrants through the New York station gradually decreased from 445,987 in 1892 to a low of 178,748 in 1898. Tragically, projections for the future needs of the immigrant receiving station in New York were based on these speciously declining figures. By 1900, with a sudden jump to 341,712 immigrants, the numbers had begun a renewed and dramatic incline.

From the start the new station, impressive as it was in appearance and final cost—$1.2 million—was woefully inadequate to meet the demands placed on it. Consequently, over the next sixteen years there had

to be numerous new constructions and remodelings, repairs and enlargements.

In 1904, just after the administration of the station was transferred from the Treasury Department to the Commerce and Labor Department, the new dining room was completed. Although it seated 150 to 200 aliens, by 1908 it had to be enlarged again to seat 1,000. Also in 1908 the Baggage and Dormitory Building, just behind the main building, was finished, and the capacity of the hospital buildings on Island 2 was doubled. A new surgeon's house and psychopathic wards were added. In the next ten years, third stories were added to the north and south wings of the main building, and the stairway from the first-floor baggage area to the second-floor processing room was shifted from the center to the far end to provide more floor space for processing. Other construction included: a third story to the Baggage and Dormitory Building, a new ferry house, an incinerator, a greenhouse, and a bakery and carpentry building. A new concrete and granite seawall was completed, and Island 3 was filled in and a Contagious Disease Hospital built on it.

In 1916 explosions set off by German saboteurs at nearby Black Tom Wharf on the Jersey shore severely damaged the Ellis Island buildings. Although no one was seriously hurt, it cost $400,000 to make repairs all over the three islands. (See Chapter 5, pages 135, 138.) The plaster vaulted ceiling in the Registry fell and was replaced by Guastavino tile.

During World War I, immigration came to a near halt, so there was no further need for building. Ellis Island was put to use by the U.S. Army and Navy. After the war, although immigration briefly resurged, it never reached its former levels. There was no more construction on Ellis until the 1930s.

CHAPTER THREE
PROCESSING

In 1907, the peak year of United States immigration, more than 1,150,000 people were admitted through Ellis Island. Even with a staff of some 350 civil servants, the station could not accommodate all who arrived in a single day. Some of the immigrants waited as long as four days on ships in the harbor. Then they were shuttled by ferry to Ellis, where it was likely that they would have to wait several more hours before there was room for them in the main building. Finally, with all their worldly belongings on their backs (right), they passed under the glass and steel entrance canopy and into the baggage room, where the processing began.

In the late nineteenth century, laws were passed that provided the basic admitting procedures that were in effect in this country for more than a generation. The law of 1891, the most comprehensive immigration regulation to date, extended and strengthened the list of alien classes to be excluded from the United States:

. . . All idiots, insane persons, paupers or persons likely to become a public charge, persons suffering from a loathsome or dangerous contagious disease, persons who have been convicted of a felony or other infamous crime or misdemeanor involving moral turpitude, polygamists, and also any person whose ticket or passage is paid for with the money of another or who is assisted by others to come, unless it is affirmatively and satisfactorily shown on special inquiry that such person does not belong to one of the foregoing excluded classes, or to the class of contract laborers: . . .

The law also made more complete provisions for the inspection and deportation of aliens and for regulation of immigration specifically from Mexico and Canada.

Several laws in 1893 expanded and refined the new restrictive measures. One prohibited the introduction of contagious or infectious diseases into the United States; ships carrying passengers with such diseases were to be quarantined. Another law stipulated for the first time that steamships provide immigration officials with manifests, or lists of aliens on board with information about each, including record of a physical examination before embarkation. A third law provided highly detailed instructions for administrative processing of immigrants (including such fine points as the manner in which their clothing and personal belongings were to have been disinfected before embarka-

tion—a provision, with several others, never to be observed in many ports). From 1891 to 1902 other miscellaneous and comparatively minor laws enlarged the duties of the Bureau of Immigration.

The staff of the new Ellis Island station, formally opened in January of 1892, consisted of about 100 federal employees, many of whom were carryovers from Castle Garden and the Barge Office. As a result of the new laws expanding the processing procedure, the small staff, according to its commissioner, was "taxed to its very limits." In his 1895 report to the Secretary of the Treasury, Commissioner Senner recommended that the Ellis Island force be expanded and that the entire Immigration Service be placed under the Civil Service. This was done in 1896 by an executive order of President Grover Cleveland. The goal was to improve the general quality of the staff, but it was some time before Civil Service criteria were applied to the Ellis Island work force. Incumbents remained on the force, and appointments continued to be made sometimes solely on the basis of the recommendations of politicians, so that the character and qualifications of the staff were variable.

Apart from federal employees, services at Ellis Island were provided by concessionaires, or private firms that contracted with the government for restaurant facilities, baggage transportation, and money exchange. In the early years of the station, these contracts were awarded to the highest bidder on the assumption that this would procure the greatest revenue for the immigrant fund. In actuality the concessionaires attempted to recoup their outlays by overcharging immigrants for services or cheating them outright. After 1896 contracts were awarded on the basis of the lowest bids: who would furnish food at the lowest price, deliver baggage at the most reasonable rates, and exchange money at the smallest percentage. In his report for 1895-96, Commissioner Senner recorded at least a fifty percent reduction in the prices charged by each of the three main concessions.

That same year the staff at Ellis was enlarged slightly in order to manage the increasing numbers of detainees. Additional night watchmen, gatemen, interpreters, and cleaners were hired on a temporary basis. The detainees, anywhere from 800 to 1,000 a night that year, were usually penniless, single men from Mediterranean countries. For lack of better facilities, they were detained outdoors in pens. On April 16, 1896, *The New York Daily Tribune* reported:

. . . Small riots that threatened to develop into trouble of a more serious nature are occurring daily among the many immigrants on Ellis Island, and the officials have become so apprehensive, that Dr. Senner yesterday telegraphed to the Treasury Department at Washington, asking permission to swear in a number of special constables to be used in keeping in subjection the unruly aliens. *The Tribune* has already told of the arrival of thousands of peasants, penniless and dirty for the most part, from the Mediterranean ports, and they are continuing to pour in daily. On Sunday the steamship *Bolivia* brought into this port 1,376 of these people, and *Alesia* followed with over one thousand. The *Werra* yesterday brought in 756 and the steamships *Victoria* and *Belgravis* are now on the way here with an aggregate of 2,820 more.

It seemed clear that many of these pitiable men were in the United States in violation of the contract labor laws (see Chapter 2, page 35), and most were deported. In response to this episode and to the increase in Italian immigration that produced it, lobbyists for immigration restriction attempted to get the first literacy test into law, but President Cleveland vetoed the bill just before he went out of office.

It had been hoped that when the immigration station was removed from the Battery to Ellis Island some of the management problems would be alleviated. Such was not the case. Commissioner Senner, himself an honest public servant, seemed unable to substantially improve processing procedures or to control corruption among his employees. His successor, Thomas Fitchie, probably equally well meaning, was also unable to do so. Both men were burdened by Assistant Commissioner Edward McSweeney, whom many observers thought was an unscrupulous character. Stories of mismanagement, graft, and mistreatment of the immigrants were published regularly, especially by the New York press, but also by the authors of popular books.

Edward Steiner, in his 1906 exposé entitled *On the Trail of the Immigrant*, publicized the worst abuses (see excerpt, Chapter 4, pages 120, 122). He made several transatlantic crossings in steerage in order to collect material for his book and reported that immigrants at Ellis Island suffered "roughness, cursing, intimidation, and a mild form of blackmail." They were served abominable food—only prunes and bread at every meal—on filthy utensils in a dining room littered with food scraps. Sometimes they were forced to work in the kitchen. During inspection, officials asked for bribes and attempted to seduce young girls. Once admitted, an immigrant was likely to be robbed of from fifty to seventy-five percent of his or her savings at the money exchange or overcharged for railroad tickets.

On a rainy fall day in 1903, a pleased-looking Teddy Roosevelt visited Ellis Island. Commissioner William Williams is to the right. Williams's reform of the station was one of the successes of the Roosevelt administration.

In the summer of 1901 a scandal involving steamships and the illegal landing of immigrants was uncovered. Fraudulent citizenship papers had been sold to aliens, allowing them to land at New York City's piers and bypass Ellis Island altogether. The money for the false papers was split among ships' officers and Ellis Island boarding inspectors. Apparently the practice had gone on for years, with as many as 10,000 aliens landed this way at five dollars each. Although Commissioner Fitchie directed an investigation, his administration was severely compromised.

President Theodore Roosevelt came into office in 1901—with his penchant for cleaning house—determined to make a clean sweep of the Immigration Bureau. Fitchie's office soon expired; McSweeney was forced to resign; and even Terence Powderly, head of the bureau in Washington, was replaced.

After several months searching for the right man to replace Fitchie as commissioner, the President chose William Williams, a young Wall Street lawyer with some government experience and a commendable record in the Spanish-American War. Williams was at first reluctant to accept the job, but Roosevelt persuaded him, assuring him that the job was "the most interesting office" he was empowered to bestow and challenging him to correct a situation in which "nearly a million immigrants a year . . . were being improperly inspected, robbed, and abused."

Williams was Commissioner of Immigration at Ellis Island for two terms, from 1902 to 1905 and from 1909 to 1913, during which he found the President's characterization that "it was a very hard office to administer" quite correct. He had not only to process huge numbers of immigrants within a limited time, space, and budget, but also to deal with a critical, muckraking

press and with the proponents of both sides of a sensitive national issue—the debate between restrictionists and antirestrictionists. He was constantly under bombardment (as were his successors in the office for the next twenty years) from members of the Immigration Restriction League (charities, law enforcement agencies, leading sociologists and biologists, organized labor, and patriotic societies), who wanted to severely limit the number and kind of immigrants admitted to the United States, and from members of the National Liberal Immigration League (ethnic societies, steamship companies, railroads, and manufacturers), who opposed any further restriction and urged the repeal of existing restrictive laws. Both groups had powerful allies in government capable of bringing pressure to bear on a commissioner whenever they disapproved of his style of administering the laws.

Twice while in office Williams was summoned to Washington to testify at investigative hearings of evidence of corruption or inhumane conditions at Ellis. (He was not the only commissioner to be so challenged. Edward Corsi, commissioner from 1931 to 1935, remarked in his own history, *In the Shadow of Liberty*, that "It would take a special volume to fully chronicle the investigations of Ellis Island and their repercussions across the nation.")

Williams accounted well for his administration at these hearings. In spite of tremendous difficulties inherent in the job of running the island station, he impressed most observers—and later historians—with his integrity and administrative skill. Within two months of taking office, he had set the tone of his administration by removing corrupt and inefficient employees, disrupting "cozy" arrangements between officials and concessionaires, and instituting various standardized administrative procedures. He soon had the following notice posted conspicuously throughout the station:

Immigrants must be treated with kindness and consideration. Any government official violating the terms of this notice will be recommended for dismissal from the Service. Any other person so doing will be forthwith required to leave Ellis Island. It is earnestly requested that any violation hereof, or any instance of any kind of improper treatment of immigrants at Ellis Island, or before they leave the Barge Office, be promptly brought to the attention of the Commissioner.

Williams did not conceal the fact that he felt the quality of immigrants coming to the United States had declined since the turn of the century, and he enforced the exclusionary clauses of the immigration laws to the fullest extent possible. The numbers of detainees and deportees increased under his administration, which provoked criticism from some ethnic societies and the foreign-language press in New York, especially the German newspapers. This was peculiar since it was not the Germans whom Williams considered inferior, being of German extraction himself. In any case, the numbers excluded at Ellis—of all nationalities—never exceeded two percent. Possibly the real instigators of the attacks on Williams's administration were the steamship companies, which advertised heavily in the foreign-language press and with which Williams was constantly embattled. He was empowered by law to levy stiff fines on the companies for transporting inadmissible aliens here, and they were obliged as well to return such aliens to their ports of origin at the companies' expense.

The exclusionary laws, in fact, became more and more specific. In 1903 a law was passed that, besides prescribing additional administrative and procedural reforms, added the following classes of aliens to the list of those to be excluded:

. . . anarchists, or persons who believe in or advocate the overthrow by force or violence of the Government of the United States or of all government or of all forms of law, or the assassination of public officials [new restriction added in the aftermath of the assassination of President William McKinley]; prostitutes, and persons who procure or attempt to bring in prostitutes or women for the purpose of prostitution; those who have been, within one year from the date of the application for admission to the United States, deported as being under offers, solicitations, promises or agreements to perform labor or service of some kind there-in. . . .

In contrast to those who felt that Williams excluded an inordinate number of admissible aliens were those who felt just as strongly that he did not exclude enough. Most vocal were those in support of strict enforcement of the contract labor laws and those concerned about the so-called "white-slave traffic." However, the 1903 law, which specifically debarred prostitutes and their procurers, provided a new means for directly confronting the traffic.

It had always been known that some prostitutes were brought into the country, and there had long been matrons in the Immigration Service trained to watch for them. But prostitutes usually came in through first- or second-class cabins, which were minimally inspected. When their procurers called for them in New York, the men were claimed to be their relatives. No one thought the problem was widespread or organized. But in 1903 the National Women's Christian Temperance Union compiled evidence that the traffic was both widespread and organized, funneling into the country through the Port of New York. The Temperance Union presented its evidence to the Secretary of the Treasury and persuaded him to appoint women immigration inspectors at Ellis Island. They would board all immigration vessels and make investigations into suspicious cases in first- and second-class cabins and give advice to those women who might have been misled into their circumstances. President Roosevelt was in favor of the operation and suspended Civil Service requirements for the five women inspectors, four of whom were social workers recommended by the Temperance Union (only one was an experienced Ellis Island attendant). Williams was skeptical and said so publicly. As a result he was criticized by a range of people who accused him of being indifferent both to decent women and to the problem of white-slave traffic.

Whether Williams and the male inspectors were justifiably resentful of the female inspectors—and of the attention they received in the press—is not known. What is known is that the experiment did not work out well. During the three-month trial period, the women inspectors caused a great many female passengers to become indignant over the highly personal questions asked them; and although they sent a number of unaccompanied young women to Ellis for special inquiry, it was not clear that they contributed substantially to the

apprehension of prostitutes. Williams reported the operation a failure, and the women inspectors were dismissed.

The Temperance Union continued lobbying, however, and was instrumental in bringing about a Civil Service class of "boarding matrons," who would board the liners and assist the male inspectors. They were instructed to act in an advisory capacity only, leaving matters of judgment to the male inspectors.

Toward the end of his first administration, Commissioner Williams prepared a summary of the various positions and duties of the staff ("Organization of the U.S. Immigration Station at Ellis Island, New York, Together With a Brief Description of the Work Done in Each of Its Divisions") as part of his report to a presidential commission then investigating reported abuses at Ellis. This document and two others that Williams prepared during his second administration ("Ellis Island: Its Organization and Some of Its Work" and "Rules for the United States Immigrant Station at Ellis Island") give an overview of how the station operated. Like most Civil Service organizations, the Ellis Island work force was divided, for the sake of efficiency, into divisions. In 1903 there were seventeen:

The Executive Division was headed by the commissioner and performed the work centering around his office. His staff consisted of an assistant commissioner, a supervising inspector, a chief clerk and numerous other clerks, an attorney, a draftsman, several stenographers and messengers, and a telephone operator. The duties of the division were supervising and coordinating the general work of all other divisions (including most administrative and legal work), considering all applications and appeals, awarding contracts,

Public Health Service attendants—only a segment of the Medical Division, which was one of many divisions within the Ellis Island work force—pose for a staff photo in front of one of the hospital buildings in 1923.

and planning and carrying out improvements to the island.

Headquartered at the Barge Office, the Boarding Division had a chief inspector and twelve others, assisted by four or five surgeons from the Medical Division and five attendants from the Matrons' Division. Their job was to board all incoming vessels at the quarantine station on Staten Island and there to inspect first- and second-class-cabin passengers. Theoretically, this inspection was the same as that received by the steerage class on Ellis. The division was to send all questionable cabin aliens to Ellis Island for further examination and to separate American citizens from the steerage so that they could land with admissible cabin passengers at the piers. They were also responsible for collecting manifests and for accompanying all immigrants going to Ellis for examination.

The Medical Division was composed of U.S. Public Health and Marine Service Hospital personnel and was divided into two parts. The smaller section was attached to the Boarding Division, and its duty was to detect diseases of a quarantinable nature—including cholera, smallpox, and yellow fever—and to send them to Public Health Service hospitals in the New York area (the Contagious Disease Hospital on Ellis was not available for occupancy for several more years). Other cases of loathsome or contagious diseases were sent to Ellis Island, where the larger part of the division, stationed at the top of the stairs in the Registry, determined, through line inspection and other tests, whether the aliens met the physical and mental requirements of the immigration laws. In the early 1900s there were about twelve doctors in the division, and these were responsible for all medical inspections and for the care of all hospitalized aliens. At the height of immigration, there were at most thirty doctors.

The Registry Division received the aliens as soon as they had successfully passed the medical inspection. These inspectors, assisted by many subordinate officials and interpreters, performed what was called the "primary" inspection, determining which aliens could land without further or special inquiry. These judgments were based on the data contained in the manifests, the aliens' answers to questions, and general impressions received. An inspector's duty was not to establish the eligibility of the applicant, but to hold for inquiry those who were not "clearly and beyond a doubt entitled to land." Only other inspectors could overrule a decision.

Inspectors from the Registry Division were assigned on a rotating basis to the Special Inquiry Division, which determined whether a detained alien would be allowed to land or be deported. Each board had three members, some of whom were appointed by the commissioner, and was assisted by interpreters, stenographers, and messengers. Usually, there were three boards in session, hearing from fifty to 100 cases each day. The Clerk of the Boards, a special office in the division, was in charge of the massive clerical work involved in trafficking aliens to and from the boards and in keeping track of the outcome of all cases.

The Information Division kept all records and was responsible for supplying interested parties with information concerning immigrants' status and whereabouts —whether landed, detained for inquiry, hospitalized, or deported.

The Discharging Division adjoined the Information Division and was in charge of aliens temporarily detained until friends or relatives called for them. After five days, if no one called, these aliens were turned over to the Special Inquiry Division.

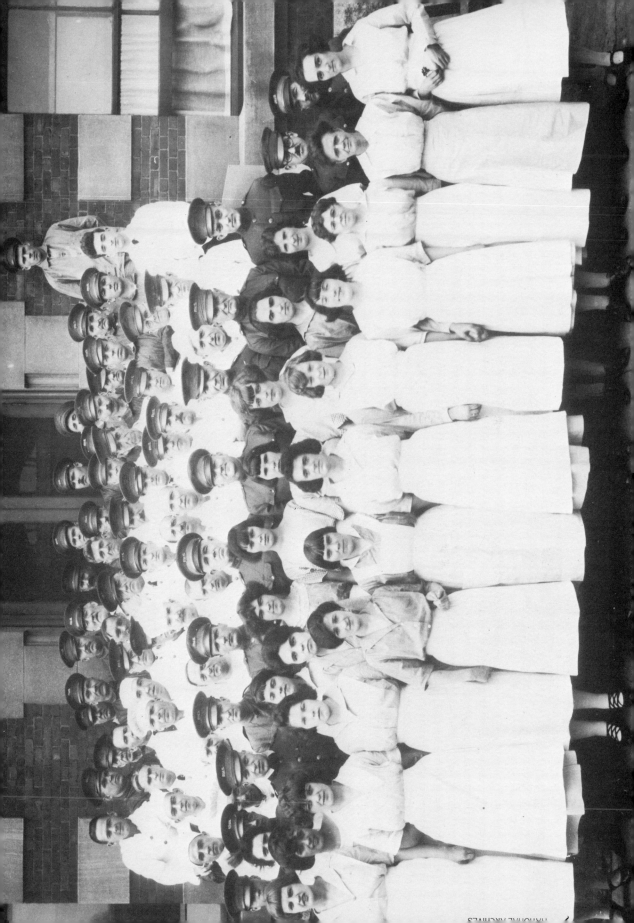

Red Cross workers serve refreshments to immigrants arriving in about 1915. Unfortunately, welcomes as warm as this were rare.

The Deportation Division—manned by a few inspectors, but mostly by clerks, watchmen, gatemen, and messengers—dealt exclusively with "deferred" aliens (those with decisions pending) and those excluded. The staff was divided into the "watch," which guarded the aliens, and the "deporting squad," which escorted them to ship.

The Statistical Division, with one chief inspector presiding over many clerks and typists, compiled all data on nationalities, races, sexes, ages, occupations, literacy, countries of origin, destinations, etc. It was from the records of this division that immigration statistics were compiled.

The clerks and bookkeepers of the Treasurer's Division prepared federal payrolls and pay checks, supervised and kept accounts of all other payments and expenditures, received numerous small sums for immigrants, routed mail, kept track of lost and found items, and kept records of all government property on the island.

The Watchmen's and Gatemen's Division was distributed among the Barge Office, the Registry floor, the Deportation Division, and the ferry and dock area. These men served as guards and "groupers," who directed traffic.

The Matrons' Division consisted of ten women, five assigned to the Boarding Division, who assisted or cared for female immigrants, particularly those with children and those held for special medical examination. Women of suspected moral character were turned over to the matrons for investigation.

The Engineers' Division operated the very elaborate heat, light, and power plant on the island, while the several dozen laborers and charwomen of the Laborers' Division kept the whole place swept, mopped, scrubbed, and disinfected. The Night Division took

over these duties after 6:00 PM, also conducting detained immigrants to dormitories in the evening and back to the appropriate detention rooms in the morning. Members of the Marine Division operated the Ellis Island tugboat, launch, and (after 1903) ferries. Carpenters, painters, laundrymen, and the gardener—who did not fit under any other category—made up the Miscellaneous Division.

The staff in 1903 numbered about 350. In later years it grew to about 500, while the number of divisions was consolidated to eleven. A report on personnel from special inspector Roger O'Donnell to the Secretary of Commerce and Labor, in which the inspector outlined ways in which the work force budget might be trimmed, gives the salary ranges in 1909. Salaries for inspectors, depending on the type of work they did, ranged from $1,200 to $2,500 a year; interpreters got $1,200 to $1,400; clerks, $900 to $2,500; carpenters, $1,600; pilots, $1,200; stenographers for boards of inquiry, $1,000; matrons, $720 to $1,400; charwomen, $800; and unskilled laborers, $720.

In addition to the staff and concessionaires, there were at various times as many as ninety different missionary and immigrant aid societies on Ellis Island. The public opinion that these were solely engaged in good works was reflected in the newspapers. In 1902 Leslie's Weekly reported: "One of the notable features of the care taken of the immigrants is the attention paid to them by the missionaries of several religious denominations and the agents of benevolent societies ...The work they are doing is of the kind that merits unstinted praise."

Commissioner Williams and his successor, Robert Watchorn, however, were more skeptical. While both men admitted that some of the societies did great good, they were on their guard against others that "paraded under false colors," using the guise actually

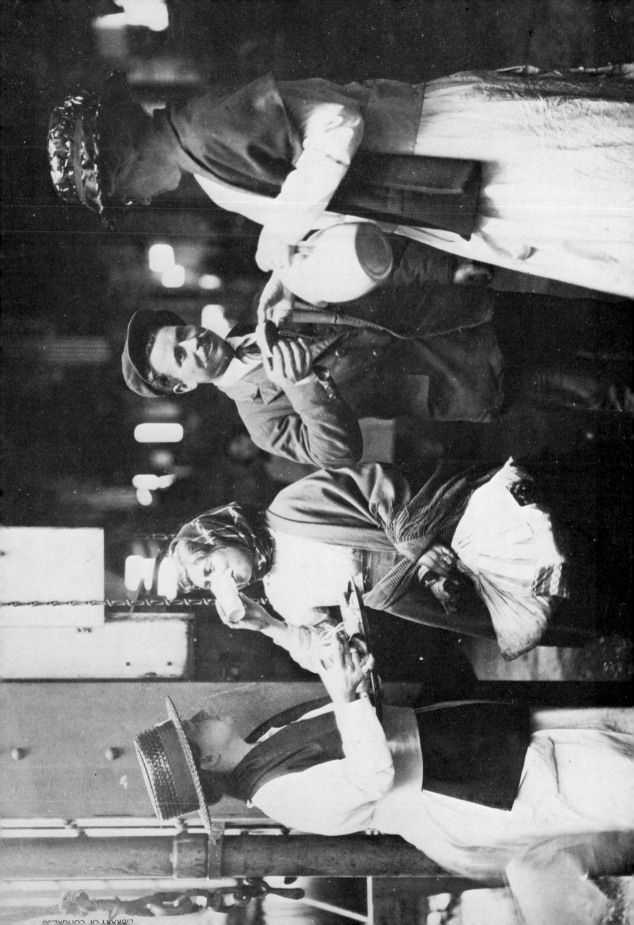

The Ellis Island tug delivers members of the Boarding Division to a newly arrived steamer. They would collect the ship's manifest, inspect first- and second-class passengers on board, then accompany steerage passengers to Ellis.

to exploit the immigrants, especially young women. Williams barred missionaries from the Registry, although he allowed them in other areas.

Watchorn carefully investigated the activities of all the societies and required them to submit monthly reports giving full data on all aliens in their care. He was opposed to excessive religious zeal on the island and warned proselytizers to stay away from Jews in particular:

A great many of our immigrants are Hebrews, who are on their way from persecution by one style of Christians, and when they have Christian tracts—printed in Hebrew—put in their hands, apparently with the approval of the United States Government, they wonder what is going to happen to them here.

The Jews in fact had their own organization, the Hebrew Sheltering and Immigrant Aid Society, later known internationally as HIAS. Originally founded in 1902 simply to provide decent burial for Jews who died at Ellis Island, the organization, under the leadership of Alexander Harkavy, soon tackled the problems of helping Jewish immigrants get a proper start in the United States. Because many Jewish immigrants would rather starve than accept nonkosher food, many arrived in the United States in a critically debilitated state. In 1911 HIAS was instrumental in having a kosher kitchen opened at Ellis. Just after the kitchen opened, nearly fifty Jews who had been scheduled for deportation were reexamined and found to be physically fit to land after all. HIAS was active on Ellis Island for over twenty years, serving meals, conducting services, finding housing and employment, and helping hundreds of thousands of Jews all over the world to locate friends and loved ones.

Robert Watchorn had been an immigrant himself

and an inspector at Ellis in the late 1890s. When he became Commissioner in 1905, he graciously acknowledged the constructive nature of the reforms instituted by his predecessor and, for the most part, continued and expanded them. Unlike Williams, however, he believed that the country could absorb as many immigrants as wanted to come here, regardless of nationality or social class, as long as they met the medical and legal requirements. He relaxed considerably the interpretation of the immigration laws, especially a rule Williams had imposed requiring each person to have a specified amount of cash on which to live until employment could be found. The rule was adjustable, depending on a person's age, physical condition, and marketable skills, ranging from ten to thirty dollars. As most detentions and deportations were on the grounds "likely to become a public charge," Watchorn's elimination of the cash stipulation led to a decline in the number of those turned away. When Williams returned to office for his second term, he reinstated the rule, and the number of deportees and detainees rose again.

Such fluctuations in the interpretation of the laws were inevitable. Although some observers criticized the seeming capriciousness with which regulations were enforced, for the most part immigrants were processed with consistency and due speed. The laws of 1891 and 1893, in effect for over two decades, set the standards: Each alien applying for admission was required to submit to a medical examination by an immigration doctor and to a legal interrogation by an inspector. The inspector was furnished with the medical report and with information from a manifest provided by the steamship company that transported the alien. On the basis of the alien's answers to questions, corroborated or not by information in the report and on

the manifest, the inspector judged the admissibility of the alien. If, in the inspector's opinion, the alien was "clearly and beyond doubt entitled to land," he or she was admitted. If not, the alien was held for investigation by a board of special inquiry. If the board upheld the negative opinion of the inspector, the alien could appeal through the Commissioner of Immigration to the Secretary of the Treasury (after 1903, to the Secretary of Commerce and Labor). The Secretary's decision was final.

In the station's early years, each vessel was required to dock at Staten Island, where it was boarded by Ellis Island inspectors. Later, after Ellis acquired its own tugboat, the inspectors boarded in mid-harbor and conducted their preliminary examination while the ship steamed into port. If there was serious contagious disease aboard, a quarantine was imposed. This caused added discomfort and frustration for those affected (sometimes entire shiploads of people), but was a necessary precaution, especially in the years when cholera, yellow fever, or typhoid was prevalent. Isolated cases of these diseases were sent to Hoffman

Island. Those who had been exposed were sent to Swinburne Island for observation. Victims of less-virulent diseases, such as measles or diphtheria, were sent to Ward's Island and other hospitals under contract in New York City; after 1911, when the facilities at Ellis were finally adequate to accommodate all sick aliens, they were sent to the Contagious Disease Hospital on Island 3.

First- and second-class passengers were inspected in the ship's saloon. An assistant surgeon general who observed the inspection process aboard the North German Lloyd steamship *Frederick der Grosse* in 1906 reported that the examination of the ship's 130 first-class-cabin and 300 second-class-cabin passengers was "very close," and perhaps for his benefit it was, but usually the inspection was limited. First class was given the most cursory examination because the steamship companies and some of the passengers themselves objected strenuously to the "insulting" questions prescribed by the law. The assumption was that anyone who could afford a first-class ticket was unlikely to become a public charge.

Second class was scrutinized a bit more carefully. Still, inspectors were looking only for cases of loathsome or dangerous contagious diseases and for passengers who might be traveling cabin class only because they knew they would not be admitted if examined at Ellis. It was quite common for a deportee to return to Europe, purchase a second-class ticket, and within three to four weeks come back to the United States. If a passenger seemed out of place in cabin class, he or she was sent to Ellis for a more thorough "line" inspection. Very few, however, were detected in this ruse.

First- and second-class passengers were discharged immediately at the piers. Steerage, or "immigrant" class, passengers were given identification cards (re-ferred to by some as "landing tickets") with numbers corresponding to their manifests. Then, if the volume of arrivals on a given day was manageable, immigrants were transferred with their baggage to smaller boats that took them to Ellis. On some days, though, there were just too many arrivals to process. The station could handle about 5,000 people during a twelve-hour workday. If more than that arrived, they had to wait on the steamers until there was room on the island. During periods of peak immigration, it was not uncommon for 10,000 to 15,000 immigrants to be waiting on ships in the harbor. Some of those people waited two days to get to Ellis Island.

The station had two ferries of its own, but these were inadequate to transport the large numbers of immigrants who arrived daily, so the steamship companies were contracted to provide additional small steamers and barges for this purpose. These were old, slow boats, and the immigrants were packed on them tightly, indoors and out, regardless of weather. Even after arrival at Ellis, they sometimes had to wait on the slip for several hours. There was no food and little drinking water; toilet facilities were few. After much argument, Commissioner Williams was eventually able to get the steamship companies to provide a little food if the landing was delayed. Watchorn, too, objected to the crowding and for a time was able to put watchmen on the ferries in an attempt to prevent it, but there was never any permanent remedy to the problem. For the most part the immigrants simply had to endure the crowding and the tedium.

Eventually an Ellis Island attendant, usually one of the watchmen or gatemen, would let the immigrants off the ferry and direct them to the canopy that led into the baggage room. Congestion in the baggage room was one of the main reasons immigrants had to wait so long for processing to begin. Every piece of luggage

Alfred Stieglitz took his famous photograph, "The Steerage," while a steamer was docked on the Hudson River. Immigrants wait below while first- and second-class passengers are landed.

The Italian family at left was photographed by Lewis Hine in 1905, just after they had boarded the ferry that would take them from the pier to Ellis Island. There they might have had to wait on the ferry for several hours before it was their turn to be processed. The men on the ferry in the photograph opposite wear their identification cards, which they will need for the processing, in their hat bands.

NATIONAL PARK SERVICE

The two gentlemen wearing hats with nautical insignia at left probably were members of the Marine Division, which operated the Ellis Island launch, tugboat, and ferries. The occupations of the other two are not immediately identifiable, although the man on the far right wears religious insignia. In the photograph opposite, a group of well-dressed women and children disembark at Ellis.

Overleaf: For most people, once the processing got started, it took no more than two or three hours. But often there were hours spent waiting beforehand—on the steamers, on the ferries, and, here, at the entrance to the baggage room.

had to be taken from the steamers onto the ferries and from the ferries into the ground-floor room of the main building, where it was stowed while the immigrants underwent processing. Afterwards it had to be trucked the entire length of the island in order to be ferried to New York or to the New Jersey railway station.

Baggage handling was one of the most profitable concessions on the island. This contract was held for nearly thirty years by the same firm, whose owner was a long-time crony of powerful New York Republicans. Stories of overcharging, slow delivery, and "lost" baggage were all too common. Frequently, when immigrants returned from line inspection to collect their baggage, they would find it ransacked, their valuables stolen. Williams considered the baggage concessionaires "importunate and contentious leeches," and

JULIAN KAISER

The ground-floor baggage room, the starting point for processing, was where immigrants stowed belongings while they underwent inspection on the floor above. It was the location, too, of the railroad ticket office, where the newly admitted arranged for their transportation farther northeast or west. Baggage handlers were not always scrupulous. On returning to the baggage room, immigrants sometimes found their belongings ransacked or missing. Lost baggage is the concern of the Italian family opposite, photographed in 1905.

both he and Commissioner Watchorn tried for years to get them off the island and to give the contract to more responsible people. As with the ferry contracts—or any issue that aroused local political/commercial opposition—the commissioners were unable to effect a permanent change, but their watchfulness did eliminate the worst abuses. Any baggage employee caught cheating an immigrant was dismissed immediately.

With baggage temporarily stored, immigrants began the first stage of processing, the medical inspection. Attendants guided them to the foot of the staircase that led to the Registry Room. At this point the immigrants were probably not even aware that the inspection had begun, but, in fact, as they walked up the stairs, sometimes carrying articles of clothing, small children, or precious belongings, the immigrants were watched by doctors at the top of the stairs. Any difficulty ascending the stairs might be seen as a sign of physical weakness and result in a more thorough examination above. In 1911, to make more room for "primary" inspection in the Registry Room, this staircase was moved to the east end of the baggage room, and the entire medical inspection was done on the first floor, but in the early years of the station, this walk up the stairs—or the "six-second medical," as it came to be called—served as a diagnostic aid for the doctors and an integral part of the inspection process.

At the top of the stairs, immigrants were met by an attendant who stamped their identification cards and directed them into a central gangway, divided by piping and wire gratings into aisles and compartments. There were two or four aisles, or "lines," depending on the volume to be processed on a given day, and at the beginning of each was an immigration doctor. The exact examination process at this point varied over the years, but based on reports submitted by commissioners, chief medical officers, and inspectors from the

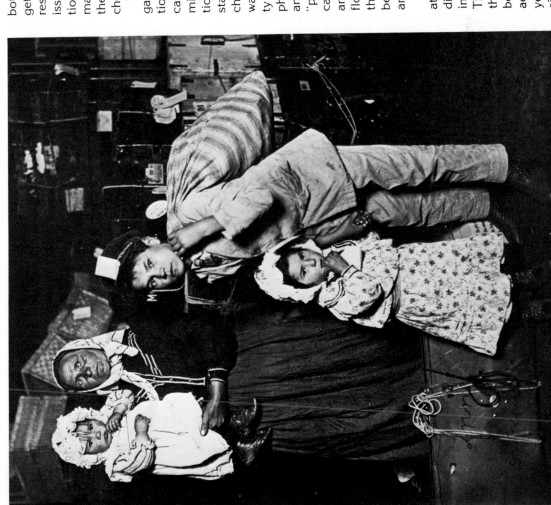

These Slavic immigrants did not know that, as they struggled with bundles up the stairs to the Registry Room, their medical examination had already begun. Doctors at the top of the stairs were watching for signs of infirmity.

Stairs to second floor, main building, summer 1982

office of the U.S. Surgeon General, the following general description can be made.

Doctors giving the general exam usually worked in pairs, one at the beginning of each line, the other about thirty feet down at a right-angle turn in the piping. Immigrants were instructed to walk slowly and to keep ten or fifteen feet apart. The doctors generally divided aspects of the examination between them, depending on their specialties and experience. They looked for all types of defects, physical and mental, observing each immigrant both straight on and in profile. They noted manner, conversation, style of dress, or any unusual appearance. Starting from the feet and working up, the doctors observed in particular each immigrant's posture and gait and the condition of the face, hands, skin, and scalp. Should some part of the body they wished to see be concealed by clothing, they would ask that the item be removed. For instance, a hat might be worn to hide an incipient scalp disease such as favus (a highly contagious fungus resulting in baldness and discoloration); a high collar might cover a goiter; a shawl over the arm might conceal a deformity or paralysis. All children over the age of two were taken from their mothers' arms and made to walk. As a matter of routine, all children's hats were removed and their scalps inspected.

A third doctor at the end of the line, the "eye man," stood with his back to a window and faced the approaching immigrant, whom he asked to stop. He spoke to the immigrant briefly to check his or her mentality, then examined the eyes for signs of optical problems or disease. Using his fingers or a special instrument for the purpose (some people said it was a button hook), he quickly everted the lids, looking particularly for trachoma, a contagious, incurable disease in which granulations under the lids cause corneal scarring, often resulting in blindness. There were many frighten-

ing rumors about this part of the examination, and most immigrants approached the eye man with fear. In truth the examination, while not pleasant, was quick and, to a person with healthy eyes, painless. In seconds the immigrant passed on, while the doctor disinfected his fingers in antiseptic solution in preparation for the next person. However, a diagnosis of trachoma could exclude an immigrant, without hope of appeal.

The doctors had two to three minutes in which to detect a loathsome or dangerous contagious disease or, more generally, any affliction that might cause the immigrant to become a public charge, including mental illness or retardation. If in doubt about anything, they marked the immigrant's shoulder with chalk: B for back; C, conjunctivitis; Ct, trachoma; E, eyes; F, face; Ft, feet; G, goiter; H, heart; K, hernia; L, lameness; N, neck; P, physical and lungs; Pg, pregnancy; Sc, scalp; S, senility; X, mental retardation; a circled X, insanity. From fifteen to twenty percent of the immigrants would get a chalk mark; some would have several.

People with chalk marks were directed into wire compartments, where they awaited further examination. This was a source of great upset and confusion for those who did not understand why they had been segregated. Entire families were held up for hours, sometimes days, when one member underwent this additional scrutiny, causing tremendous anguish and frustration.

As soon as possible—usually during intervals between the arrivals of the barges—immigrants who had been detained for further medical examination were seen by doctors. There were separate examining rooms for males and females, and the rooms for females were attended by matrons. Sometimes, of course, the examination resulted in immediate clearance, and the immigrant was allowed to rejoin his or her family, but more often—because the doctors were

Halfway through the medical examination, a woman and her children are questioned by the second doctor on the line. Further down, with his back to the light from the open door, is the "eye man."

The transatlantic crossing was hard on babies; many arrived ill or became ill soon after landing. In 1909, 1,506 babies were treated on Ellis Island for measles, scarlet fever, and diphtheria; 205 died. Commissioner Williams had the temperatures of all detained children under the age of twelve taken every day in order to detect and isolate cases as soon as possible.

In the photo opposite, an immigration doctor uses a special instrument (some said it was a button hook) to evert a young woman's eyelid. He is looking for trachoma. The majority of all medical deportees had this blinding disease.

really very practiced at recognizing symptoms—the illness or disability was confirmed. The ill were sent to the hospital, where many recovered and resumed their journeys.

Angelo Pellegrini, who emigrated with his parents from Italy, wrote of his stay at Ellis:

We lived there for three days—Mother and we five children, the youngest of whom was three years old. Because of the rigorous physical ex-

amination that we had to submit to, particularly of the eyes, there was this terrible anxiety that one of us might be rejected. And if one of us was, what would the rest of the family do? My sister was indeed momentarily rejected; she had been so ill and had cried so much that her eyes were absolutely bloodshot, and Mother was told, 'Well, we can't let her in.' But fortunately, Mother was an indomitable spirit and

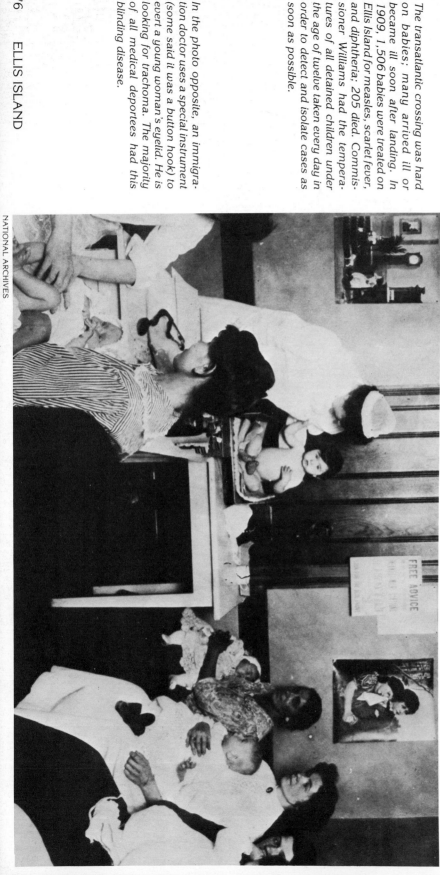

In separate rooms for men and women, immigrants who had been marked for closer inspection were examined by the doctors. Matrons were to watch for pregnant unmarried women, as these were likely to "become a public charge."

NATIONAL ARCHIVES

The man with "K" chalked on his collar is to be examined for a suspected hernia. Early in his first administration, Commissioner Williams, anxious to tighten medical inspection, directed that unmarried men be examined for venereal disease. As this was time-consuming and the incidence proved to be low, he discontinued the practice, except for occasional spot checks.

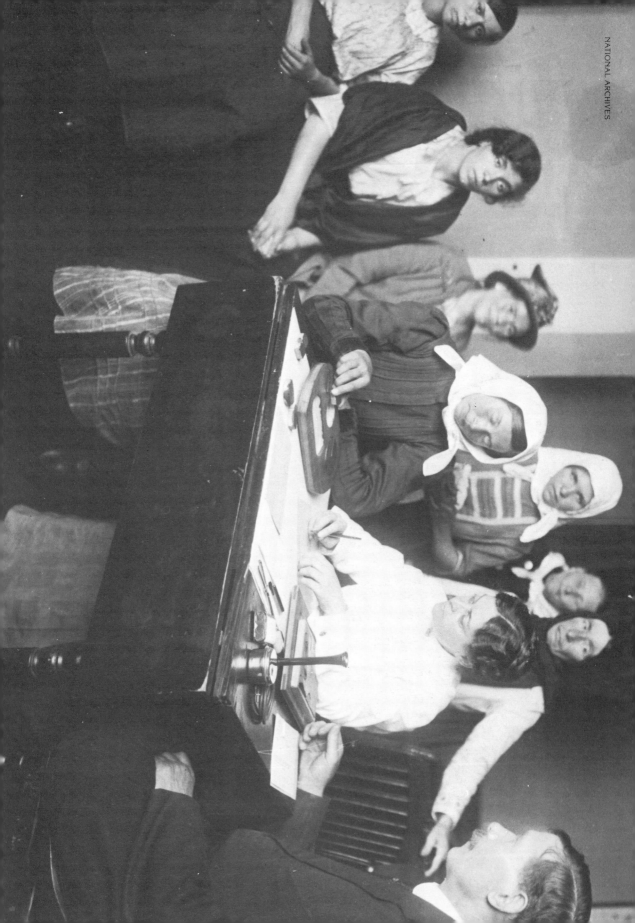

The woman here is taking a "form board" type of psychological performance test, in which she is to sort shapes into their matching slots. With the institution of standardized tests in 1914, the number of immigrants certified mentally defective jumped eighty-nine percent from the previous year.

Overleaf: With benefit of strong sunlight, nurses are giving these amused children a "head check." Pediculosis, or head lice, was endemic. Immigrants were supposedly deloused by the steamship companies before they left ports of origin. Regardless, the process often had to be repeated at Ellis.

finally made them understand that if her child had a few hours' rest and a little bite to eat she would be all right. In the end we did get through. (From *Destination America*, by Maldwyn A Jones.)

Sometimes, however, the unfortunate detainee fit within one of the classes debarred by law. The most commonly excluded diseases were: trachoma, tuberculosis in its many forms, favus, ringworm and other parasitic diseases, leprosy, venereal disease, and amoebic dysentery. Other diseases that might affect a person's ability to work were sometimes (depending on other considerations) excludable: hernia, heart disease, malnutrition, deformity, varicosity, arthritis, and poor vision. Victims of one of these diseases went before one of the special medical boards, staffed only by medical officers, or before a "board of special inquiry." If not cleared for admission, they were likely to be deported within a few days.

In 1912 *Popular Science Monthly* reported medical statistics at Ellis Island for 1911: Of the 637,003 immigrants processed for entry that year, 1,361 were certified for loathsome or dangerous contagious diseases, of which eighty-five percent had trachoma. Over 6,000 were treated at the hospital on the island and another 720 at the State Quarantine Hospital. There were 100 deaths in quarantine, mainly from measles, scarlet fever, and meningitis. The article does not report the number of deaths on Ellis, but going by other years, it was probably around 200. (Bodies not claimed by families were collected by an undertaker under contract; most were buried in Brooklyn.)

Special effort was made to detect idiots, imbeciles, epileptics, the feeble-minded, the senile, and the insane—all excludable by law. During inspection "inattentive" or "stupid-looking" aliens would be asked in the various languages to state age, destination, and nationality or to do simple sums or multiplication. Failure to answer correctly was sufficient to have an immigrant marked "X" and detained for mental examination. In addition, talkativeness, impudence, eroticism, boisterousness, surliness, apparent intoxication, confusion, aimlessness, tremulousness, stuttering, disorientation—even excessive friendliness—were considered symptomatic of abnormal mentality.

Any immigrant behaving strangely was sent to the "mental room," where he or she was questioned more carefully and observed for a while by medical officers to see if testing was warranted. If so, the immigrant was held for twenty-four hours, then given a third examination that included further questioning and, after 1913, a few psychological and neurological tests. This "weeding out" process generally found at least a few immigrants ineligible for admission each month. For example, a public health officer reported that in June 1916, of the 11,465 steerage passengers inspected at Ellis, 1,219 got an "X" chalk mark; of these 974 were released on the same day of arrival and 245 were held over for testing; after testing, 36 were certified mentally defective.

The medical inspectors at Ellis bore an overwhelming responsibility in determining the state of health of as many as 5,000 immigrants daily, and their opinions led to a great many deportations. But it must be noted that the doctors themselves did not have the power to exclude. They simply issued certificates of health or abnormality and sent the immigrants on their way to the next phase of inspection.

After the medical part of line inspection, immigrants were directed to the main-floor area of the Registry Room and into aisles that led to the "primary," or legal, inspectors. Special gatemen, or groupers, checked

The *Marine Hospital* on Ellis, at right, staffed by thirty physicians who also rotated on line work, was a well-run, efficient operation. In 1914, 10,485 immigrants were treated for a diversity of defects, ailments, and injuries. Their treatment was made difficult, according to Acting Commissioner Byron Uhl, "by the many languages spoken and the most appalling ignorance and superstition of many of the patients." The patients opposite with their heads wrapped in bandages were detained for treatment of favus, the most common of several "loathsome" scalp diseases imported from southern Europe. If they were cured, these children would be admitted.

Each year

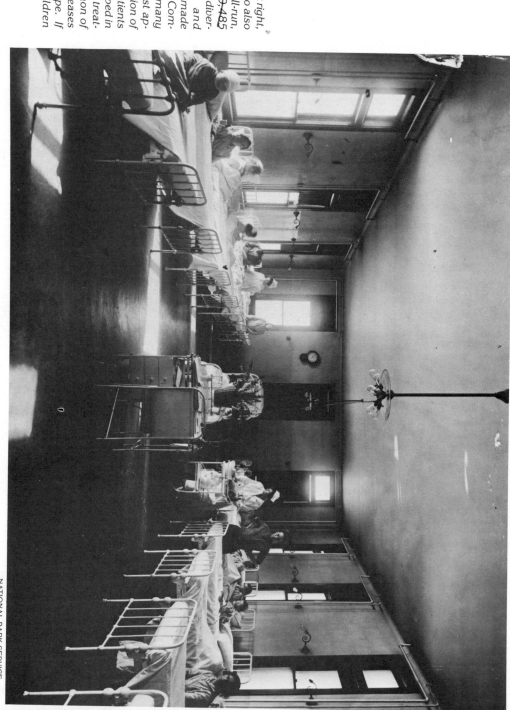

Hospital buildings, Islands 2 and 3, summer 1982

JULIAN KAISER

Wheelchair and crutches, main building, fall 1984; medicine bottles, Contagious Disease Hospital, spring 1985

JULIAN KAISER

identification cards to make sure that each immigrant got on the line that led to the inspector who had the manifest with his or her name on it. Because of limited floor space, there never were more than about twenty inspectors and lines, so on days when there were many arrivals, progress was slow. In the early years of the station, immigrants stood the whole time or sat on their bundles, but during his administration Commissioner Watchorn had the aisle railings removed and benches installed so the immigrants could sit while they waited.

BARBARA BENTON

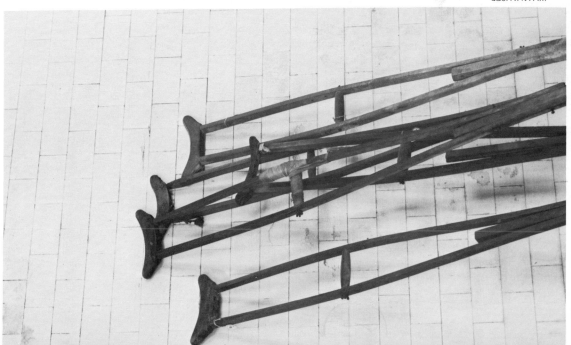

JULIAN KAISER

The forty-six-star American flag hanging from the balcony indicates that this photograph of the Registry Room was taken sometime between 1907 and 1912. Benches had replaced the iron railings leading to the inspection desks.

At the head of each line was an inspector and an interpreter. Unless the immigrant spoke English—or the inspector spoke the immigrant's language—the interpreter did the questioning (at one time the station had interpreters fluent in thirty languages). He was an important assistant to the inspector, whose job was to determine whether an immigrant was "clearly and beyond a doubt entitled to land." By law, he was required to corroborate specific information on the manifest. He asked the immigrant for his or her:

1. Full name
2. Age
3. Sex
4. Whether married or single
5. Calling or occupation
6. Whether able to read or write
7. Nationality
8. Last residence
9. Seaport for landing in the United States
10. Final destination in the United States
11. Whether having a ticket through to such final destination
12. Whether the immigrant paid his own passage or whether it had been paid by other persons, or by any corporation, society, municipality, or government
13. Whether in possession of money; and, if so, whether upward of $30, and how much if $30 or less
14. Whether going to join a relative; and, if so, what relative, and his name and address
15. Whether ever before in the United States; and, if so, when and where
16. Whether ever in prison, or almshouse, or supported by charity
17. Whether a polygamist
18. Whether under contract, express or implied, to perform labor in the United States
19. The immigrant's condition of health, mental and physical, and whether deformed or crippled; and, if so, by what cause.

Unless they had been coached at home or during the crossing, the immigrants found many of these questions incomprehensible. A big problem was the fine line between having reasonable prospects for employment and being a contract laborer. Some had been told to be friendly and answer yes to everything. Others were prepared to bribe the inspector. Some, in their fear and misapprehension, gave entirely wrong information about themselves or, in the confusion of language, were misunderstood. In spite of this, the questioning was over in two or three minutes, and about eighty percent got through.

The other twenty percent were detained in order to be questioned more carefully by a "board of special inquiry." Each board (there were usually five to eight in session every day) consisted of three appointed members, usually at least one of whom had experience on the line. Rarely did any of the members have legal training, but they were supervised by the station's legal staff.

Immigrants appearing before the boards were by no means treated like United States citizens. They were not allowed to have lawyers or to talk to friends and relatives until the board had made a decision. Board members conducted the inquiry in whatever manner

they thought would elicit the truth, and the decision of any two members prevailed. Although an immigrant could appeal through the Commissioner of Immigration to the Secretary of the Treasury (or, later, of Commerce and Labor), if the Secretary did not waive the board's decision, the immigrant had no recourse but to take the next ship back to his native country. A federal judge in New York, hearing an appeal attempted through the courts, was to remark, "if the Commissioners wish to order an alien drawn, quartered, and chucked overboard, they could do so without interference."

Certain classes of people were explicitly excluded by law—contract laborers, criminals, etc.—and usually in these cases the law was vigorously enforced. After 1903 medical certificates from the immigration doctors for certain diseases were also binding. But there were many cases that fell within a vast gray area in the law, and these had to be considered individually.

The real issue before a board of inquiry was whether or not a person was "likely to become a public charge." If detained for medical reasons, the question was whether the immigrant could be expected to recover sufficiently from the disability in order to avoid becoming a charity case. If the detainee was the head of a household with limited funds, the board had to decide the likelihood of his finding employment before funds ran out. Unaccompanied married women, with or without children, were required to give proof that a responsible male family member awaited them. Unaccompanied children under the age of twelve and single women had to wait on the island until relatives picked them up.

Most board decisions were tempered by humane considerations, and the immigrant usually got the benefit of the doubt. No more than about two percent of the total number of immigrants in one year were

At the heads of long lines in the Registry were the inspection desks, manned by primary inspectors and interpreters who would ask immigrants a list of questions prescribed by current law. An Italian man is about to have his turn with the inspector. After hours of waiting, in a matter of minutes he will be officially landed, temporarily detained, or sent before a board special inquiry for further questioning.

Overleaf: A group of British women, haberdashery remarkably preserved during the voyage in steerage, evidently do not appreciate the humor of watchmen, or "groupers," who will see to it that they get on the correct line.

JULIAN KAISER

ever actually deported. Naturally, there were some in-consistencies in the way decisions were made, and the public and press were ever ready to protest what seemed alternately a heavy-handed or a too-lax policy.

President Theodore Roosevelt, under pressure from Jewish constituents, once wrote to Commissioner Williams that, although he was in favor of deporting any undesirable, "...we must remember that to send him back is often to inflict a punishment upon him only less severe than death itself, and in such cases we must be sure not merely that we are acting aright but that we are able to show others that we are acting aright."

President Taft once involved himself in a few cases that aroused his sympathy, but he later told a New York

Those who were not "beyond a doubt entitled to land"—in most cases because inspectors felt they were "likely to become a public charge"—were held for special inquiry by boards of inspectors who decided each case on its merits. Although many immigrants were delayed by this procedure, only about two percent were actually deported.

NEW YORK PUBLIC LIBRARY

Sun reporter: "I have since followed these cases in which I influenced [Commissioner Williams] against his better judgment, and I am obliged to make the humiliating confession to you that the outcome vindicated him and showed that my judgment was at fault for lack of experience."

Detainees, held over for varying lengths of time (rarely more than two weeks) until their cases could be decided, were housed, fed, and given medical care at no cost to themselves. Statistics on detentions are fragmentary for the years of peak immigration, 1900 to 1915, but temporary detentions—of those awaiting funds or relatives, for instance—were the most numerous, followed by detentions for legal considerations and, further down the scale, detentions for hospitalization.

Facilities during those years were almost always strained to the limit. Dormitories designed for about 1,500 persons often housed 2,500. Hospital buildings, too, were packed to capacity. Commissioner Watchorn complained that the crowding was an "intolerable situation...which no private corporation would have permitted to continue for a single day if the laws relating to health and decent comfort in any city of the United States had been applied to it." He and Commissioner Williams were constantly pleading with Washington for additional funds for improvements and enlargements, and construction of some sort was always in progress (see Chapter 2, page 47). Ironically, by the time the Ellis Island facilities had been upgraded to a degree approaching adequacy, the outbreak of World War I curtailed immigration, and the influx never again approached the levels of those years.

Detainees at Ellis passed the time as best they could. There was no entertainment, and movement was confined to a rooftop exercise area. There was a playground for the children and a "religious" room set aside for observances of all denominations, its stained-glass windows lending an appropriate reverential atmosphere.

Before Commissioner Williams instituted reforms in 1902, the restaurant had been one more area in which immigrants had been cheated and mistreated by concessionaires. After Williams revoked the contract and relet it, with new rules, to a different firm, the food was nutritious, if plain, consisting mainly of thick soups and stews, boiled vegetables and fruits, and breads. People's food preferences, not to mention dietary laws, were difficult to accommodate. Italians, for instance, complained about the lack of wine; a group of Moham-

JULIAN KAISER

medan dervishes, forbidden to eat food over which the shadow of an infidel had passed, lived on boiled eggs. But no one starved.

A menu for one day might have been:

Breakfast—boiled eggs, coffee, bread and butter, milk;

Dinner—beef broth with barley, boiled beef, vegetables, boiled potatoes, sour pickles, tapioca pudding, coffee, bread and butter, milk;

Supper—corned beef hash with green peppers, blackberry jelly, tea or coffee, bread and butter, milk.

Immigrants were also able to buy box lunches for a few cents to take with them when they left the island.

Dining room and pantry, summer 1982

The quality of the meals and service in the restaurant varied from abominable to quite good over the years, depending on the holder of the food contract. Commissioner Curran attempted to have ethnic foods served for a while, but quickly reverted to the standard American fare, commenting that the immigrants would have to get used to it soon anyway.

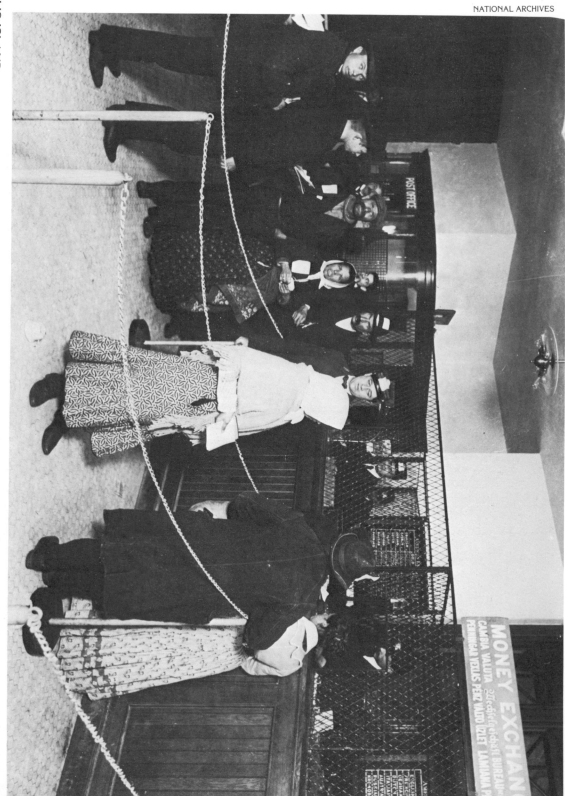

When immigrants were finished with processing in the Registry, those who had been admitted were sent back downstairs, where various services were available to them. They could change foreign currency to American money, send telegrams and letters, purchase railway tickets, or seek the advice of one of the immigrant-aid societies.

JULIAN KAISER

RAILROAD TICKETS to ALL POINTS
EISENBAHN BUREAU
JÆRNBANE BILLET KONTOR
VASUTI JEGYEK
BIGLIETTI FERROVIARII
ZELESNICKI KARTI

After immigrants had been admitted, they were directed back downstairs to the social services area. Here many availed themselves of the services offered by missionaries and immigrant aid societies, which helped to locate relatives and to find work and lodgings. Many sent or received telegrams. Until Commissioner Williams devised an inexpensive postcard that announced a person's arrival at Ellis and advised the recipient that he or she could call for the immigrant without incurring any expense, the two telegraph companies that operated stations on the island did an annual volume of around 30,000 telegrams. After the postcard was put in use, this number dropped, as did the incidence of overcharging for the service.

After admission, money changing, too, was a necessity. Commissioner Williams estimated that in peak years immigrants brought close to $20 million in foreign money into the United States. The opportunity for cheating immigrants by changing money at fraudulent rates was more than the original concessionaire could resist—immigrants were lucky to receive fifty percent of their money's value. In his general housecleaning in 1902, Williams fired this firm and relet the contract to the American Express Company, after which business was conducted at a fair rate of exchange.

The next step for immigrants headed farther west or northeast was the railroad ticket office, located in the rear of the baggage room. Virtually all railroad and coastal steamship companies with terminals in greater New York, Jersey City, and Hoboken had representatives who transacted multimillion-dollar business on Ellis Island, and they were a powerful aggregation. In his usual combative style, Williams took them on. When he learned that immigrants were being ticketed at first-class rates for third-class ("emigrant") accommodations and then given overly long, circuitous

After admission, immigrants line up for railway tickets.

After purchasing a railway ticket like the one here, good in "emigrant cars" only (somehow it seemed that most destinations were by way of Chicago), an immigrant was tagged, opposite, so he or she would not get lost en route.

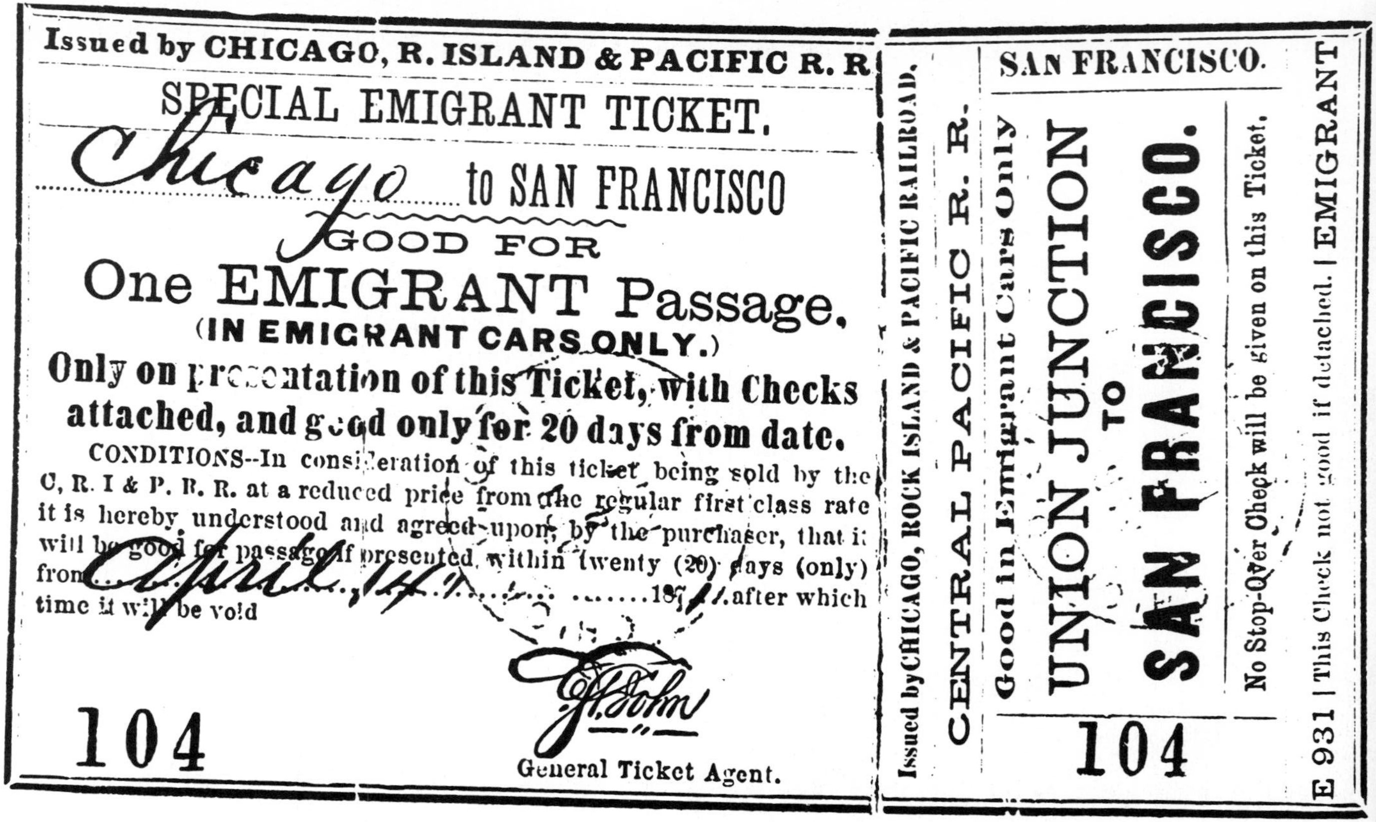

Issued by CHICAGO, R. ISLAND & PACIFIC R. R.

SPECIAL EMIGRANT TICKET.

Chicago ...... GOOD FOR ...... to SAN FRANCISCO

One EMIGRANT Passage,
(IN EMIGRANT CARS ONLY.)

Only on presentation of this Ticket, with checks attached, and good only for 20 days from date.

CONDITIONS—In consideration of this ticket being sold by the C, R. I & P. R. R. at a reduced price from the regular first class rate, it is hereby understood and agreed upon by the purchaser, that it will be good for passage if presented within twenty (20) days (only) from .... 195.. after which time it will be void.

104

General Ticket Agent.

Issued by **CHICAGO, ROCK ISLAND & PACIFIC RAILROAD.**

CENTRAL PACIFIC R. R.

SAN FRANCISCO.

Good in Emigrant Cars Only

UNION JUNCTION TO SAN FRANCISCO.

104

No Stop-Over Check will be given on this Ticket.

E 931 | This Check not good if detached. | EMIGRANT

routes to their eventual destinations—to the profit of the transportation companies—he issued an office order directing that immigrants be ticketed directly to their destinations. He especially forbade layovers in New York City, where the immigrants regularly fell "in" to the hands of unscrupulous people. Anyone, whether an official, privilege holder, or any other person at the station violating [those] terms...[would] be severely dealt with." In addition, Williams sent inspectors incognito onto the trains to check on conditions. Any

railroad mistreating its passengers was "requested to show cause why it should not improve its methods, or be relieved of its privileges at Ellis Island." Williams's impact on the operations of the transportation companies probably was but slight. Doubtless he was able to better the travel conditions for at least some immigrants. Robert Watchorn also attempted ticket price reform with questionable success. He was able to get the railroad companies to build separate terminals for immigrants in New Jersey.

For immigrants bound only for Manhattan, the New York Room was the scene of many happy reunions, as they met friends and family there. A government ferryboat delivered them, with baggage, to the Barge Office.

What was it like to be an immigrant "processed" through Ellis Island? Most felt like cattle or some other commodity being sorted for consumption. Stephen Graham, a British author who emigrated from Liverpool in 1913, wrote in *With Poor Immigrants to America:* "It is not good to be like a hurrying, bumping, wandering piece of coal being mechanically guided to sacks of its type and size, but such is the lot of the immigrant at Ellis Island."

What was it like to work at Ellis? Fiorello LaGuardia, later mayor of New York City, worked as an interpreter at the station for a number of years. He recorded in his autobiography, *The Making of an Insurgent:*

On the whole, the personnel of the Immigration Service was kindly and considerate. At best, the work was an ordeal. Our compensation, besides our salaries, for the heartbreaking scenes we witnessed, was the realization that a large percentage of these people pouring into Ellis Island would probably make good and enjoy a better life than they had been accustomed to where they came from.

Without a doubt, during the peak years of immigration, conditions at Ellis Island were at many times miserable for immigrants and administrators alike. Thomas Pitkin, former historian for the National Park Service and author of an administrative history of Ellis Island, *Keepers of the Gate,* gives a fair summary: "...Once the pattern of politics and corruption had been broken in 1902, [Ellis Island] probably was run as efficiently, as honestly, and with as much consideration for the immigrants as its overwhelming problems and the frailty of human nature would permit."

Opposite and overleaf: Those going to New York caught the Ellis Island ferry on one of its many runs back to the Barge Office. From there, they were on their own in America.

CHAPTER FOUR
PEOPLE

The immigrants at left, crowded on the deck of a liner entering New York harbor in 1906, were a fraction of the 880,036 who passed through Ellis Island that year. The dominant nationalities during the first decade of the century were English, Irish, Scandinavian, German, Polish, Russian, "Hebrew," Slovakian (sleeping woman above), Croatian and Slovenian, Italian, Greek, and "Magyar," with the greatest numbers from eastern and southern Europe. Their stories are best told in their own words or by contemporaries.

This group of Slavic women were very likely to have been joining their menfolk in one of the mining states, such as Pennsylvania. The elaborate labels probably are either identification cards given on board ship or railway passes acquired after processing at Ellis.

The immigrant experience of America began with the first sighting of land. The impact of arrival on a group of Italians was described by journalist Broughton Brandenburg in *Imported Americans* in 1903. Brandenburg and his wife lived for a time in the Italian quarter of New York, then in Italy, where they disguised themselves as immigrants and traveled by steerage back to America. The material for Brandenburg's book, which was intended to be an exposé, appeared first as a series of magazine articles.

The night before, the joy among the emigrants that they were reaching the Promised Land was pitiful to see, mingled as it was with the terrible dread of being debarred.

There was little sleeping all night. About twelve o'clock the women woke up the sleeping children, opened their packs, and took out finery on top of finery, and began to array the little ones to meet their fathers. My wife pleaded with Camela [a fellow passenger] to stay in her bunk and wait for daylight at least, but Camela could not understand why she should wait, and at three o'clock little Ina was brought up on deck arrayed in her very best, and as clean as her mother could make her with a small bottle of water and a skirt [used as a] combination wash-rag and towel.

By six o'clock all the baggage in the compartments had been hauled out and up on deck, and the hundreds of emigrants were gathered there, many trying to shave, others struggling for water in which to wash, and mothers who had been unable to dress their children to their satisfaction in the cramped quarters below were doing the job all over again, despite the chill air.

Happy, excited, enthusiastic as they were, there was still that dread among the people of the 'Batteria,' the name used to sum all that pertains to Ellis Island. I saw more than one man with a little slip of notes in his hand carefully rehearsing his group in all that they were to say when they came up for examination, and by listening here and there I found that hundreds of useless lies were in preparation. Many, many persons whose entry into the country would be in no way hindered by even the strictest enforcement of the letter of the emigration laws, were trembling in their shoes, and preparing to evade or defeat the purpose of questions which they had heard would be put to them. . . .

As we approached Sandy Hook the alternate glee and depression of the groups were pathetic. . . .

Slowly we steamed down the river in midafternoon, and when we reached the slip at Ellis Island we merely tied up, for there were many barge-loads ahead of us, and we waited our turn to be unloaded and examined. . . .

Waiting, waiting, waiting, without food and without water; or, if there was water, we could not get to it on account of the crush of people. Children cried, mothers strove to hush them, the musically inclined sang or played, and then the sun went down while we waited and still waited. . . .

The babies had sobbed themselves to sleep, worn-out mothers sat with their heads dropped on the children they held to their breasts, and among the men mirth and song had died away, though now and then a voice

In 1902 Ernest Hamlin Abbott, a writer for *Outlook* magazine, reacted very positively to the processing at Ellis Island. His article, "America's Welcome to the Immigrant," which described the receiving station as ugly but the treatment of the immigrants as tender and charitable, followed the progress of a group of Italians after landing. Abbott obviously was one observer who was impressed by the administration of Ellis Island and by its social service organizations.

At a distance, apparently rising from the surface of the water in the middle of the harbor, were some grayish-looking buildings. As they came nearer into view they grew reddish. It was plain that they were of brick, with gray stone trimmings. They were very ugly. The treeless strip of land upon which, as it could now be seen, they rested was Ellis Island, the New York station of the United States Immigration Service under the Treasury Department. Towering high above these buildings, but on another island, separated by a narrow channel, stood the gigantic bronze Statue of Liberty. The greenish-white verdigris that streaked the huge goddess bore witness to her indifference to weather as she symbolizes the freedom which the thousands who pass her shrine are seeking. When the ferryboat had at last entered the slip and was made fast, the passengers streamed out. . . .

would be heard inquiring if any one knew when or where we would get something to eat.

'All ready for the last *Irenes*,' sang out a voice somewhere in the darkness up by the buildings, and there was a clatter of feet overhead and on the wharf. The doors of the barge were opened. The barge hands dragged out the plank. The ropes restraining the crowd were dropped, and the weary hundreds, shouldering their baggage yet once again, poured out of the barge on to the wharf. Knowing the way, I led those of our group who were with my wife and myself straight to the covered approach to the grand entrance to the building, and the strange assemblage of Old World humanity streamed along behind us, an interesting procession indeed. . . .

Half-way up the stairs an interpreter stood telling the immigrants to get their health tickets ready, and so I knew that Ellis Island was having 'a long day' and we were to be passed upon even if it took half the night. . . .

If the first building which the immigrant encounters after landing is not beautiful, it is at least clean. At the end of the passageway is a sort of transept in which is what seemed to be a labyrinth of iron latticework and railings. At one end, near some benches, and seated at work at a desk, was a representative of the Society for the Protection of Italian Immigrants. From his first word of greeting to the end, as he acted as guide and interpreter in conversations with the immigrants, he gave evidence of an unaffected personal care for the individual difficulties and needs with which he had to deal—that human feeling which the King James Version calls 'charity.' Indeed, it was amazing to see how, in spite of the routine that is necessary in managing hundreds and sometimes thousands every day, each official seemed actuated by the human more than the professional motive.

An Italian woman and her tired children wait outside the baggage room for processing to begin. From 1901 to 1910 some 1.7 million southern Italians came to the United States—by far the greatest number of any nationality; another 342,000 came from northern Italy.

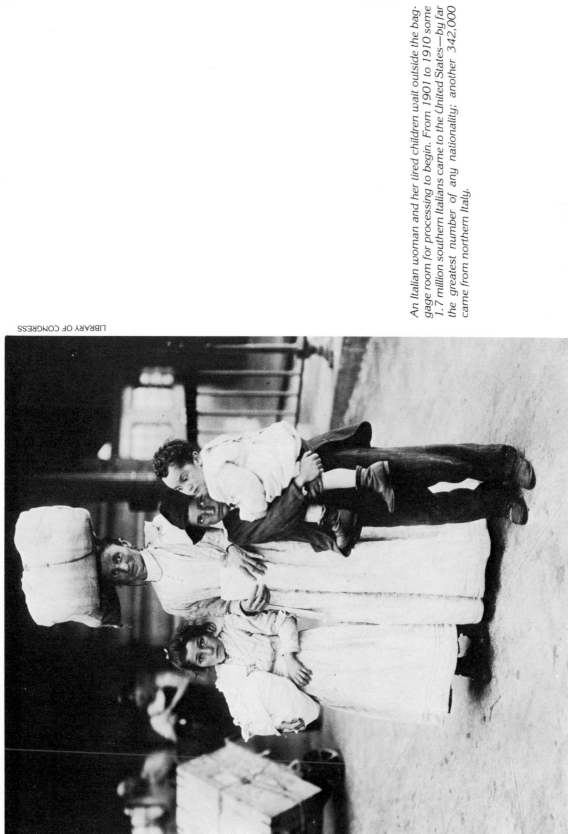

There was a small but steady stream of Blacks through Ellis Island: from 1900 to 1920, about 100,000 were admitted, most from the Caribbean.

The visitor to Ellis Island would have to be of very callous heart not to be conscious of the real tenderness with which helplessness is there treated. . . .

It was about noon when the announcement was made that a boatload of Italian immigrants that had been transferred from a steamer just come to port was landing at the island. Along the wharf they came trudging, the men staggering along with heavy bags and bundles in their hands, the women either carrying children in their arms or walking along upright and steady under the weight of bundles on their heads. The great hall on the second floor, all marked off into passageways by railings, was ready for their arrival. The doctors, detailed by the army for this work, were standing in position with their hands already dipped into antiseptic. Up the stairs came the immigrants in single file—turned to the right past one doctor, then, passing another doctor, turned to the right again. The trained eye of the physician in most cases was satisfied with a glance. Now and then, however, he would examine the eye of a man or woman, turning the lid back with his skillful fingers. One old man, as he came along, he turned by a motion into a cage at his right. The man looked hungrily, but in vain, for some sign of relenting from the officer.

The others were sorted out—those whose names appeared together on the same manifest being kept together. Each group was sent past an inspector who verified the statements made on the manifests filled out by the steamship company. There was no time for leisure. The inspector rattled off his questions

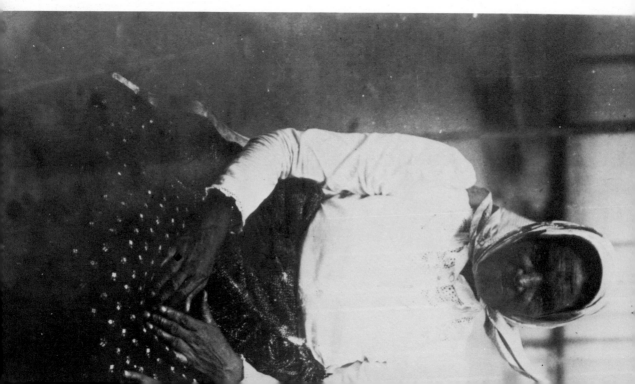

sharply in Italian; the immigrants, crowding closely and leaning forward, anxiety depicted in every face, answered breathlessly....

And so the lines passed, the inspectors outwardly gruff, but every now and then smiling at some little incident that amused them or excited their sympathy. Of the immigrants who had passed the lines, some were buying their railway tickets at a window, others changing money at another. Some were going down the staircase to the right to the room where the railway companies had their agents, passing on their way the lunch counter, where for very small sums they might buy good food for their long journeys. The immigrant aid society there has an opportunity for assisting them in their purchases. Down the staircase to the left were going others who likewise were not detained, but instead of continuing their journey by rail were to remain in New York. It is only among this class of immigrants, independent and self-reliant, that the victims of the padrones and the runners are to be found. Those who were going down the middle staircase, to be either temporarily detained or finally excluded, had the best protection. To the alien who comes to America the surest defense is defenselessness; his greatest protection is his weakness. He will be released only when the Government has evidence that he will be cared for....

Downstairs the agent of the Italian immigrant society was hastening back and forth through the corridors, seeing that the immigrants were delivered safely into the hands of their friends. His work involved an

elaborate system of record in books and on cards. After much calling of names and asking of questions, a woman was allowed to receive her sister-in-law, with considerable kissing; a stalwart, middle-aged man was happily put in charge of his pretty-faced grand-daughter; a rough-looking laborer was permitted to meet his sister. At last the cards of this group of visitors were all accounted for....

Edward Steiner, who had come through Castle Garden in the old days, was much less favorably impressed than Abbott by Ellis Island. Like the Brandenburgs, Steiner traveled by steerage to America in order to collect material for his book, *On the Trail of the Immigrant*, published in 1906. He thought the processing was mechanical and superficial.

Mechanically and with quick movements we were examined for general physical defects and for the dreaded trachoma, an eye disease, the prevalence of which is greater in the imagination of some statisticians than it is on board immigrant vessels.

From here we pass into passageways made by iron railings, in which only lately, through the intervention of a humane official, benches have been placed, upon which closely crowded, we await our passing before the inspectors.

Already a sifting process has taken place; and children who clung to their mother's skirts have disappeared, families have been divided, and those remaining intact, cling to each other in a really tragic fear that they may share the fate of those previously examined....

Most immigrants put on their finest clothing for their arrival in America. One photographer observed, "At times the Island looked like a costume ball with the multicolored, many-styled national costumes." This Hungarian woman probably made her four daughters their matching dresses; her own skirt is intricately embroidered.

The average immigrant obeys mechanically; his attitude towards the inspector being one of the greatest respect. While the truth is not always told, many of the lies prepared proved both inefficient and unnecessary.

The examination can be superficial at best; but the eye has been trained and discoveries are made here, which seem rather remarkable. . . .

Four ways open to the immigrant after he passes the inspector. If he is destined for New York he goes straightaway down the stairs, and there his friends await him if he has any; and most of them have. If his journey takes him westward, and there the largest percentage goes, he enters a large, commodious hall to the right, where the money-changers sit and the transportation companies have their offices. If he goes to the New England states he turns to the left into a room which can scarcely hold those who go to the land of the pilgrims and puritans. The fourth way is the hardest one, taken by those who have received a ticket marked P.C. (Public Charge), which sends the immigrant to the extreme left where an official sits, in front of a barred gate behind which is the dreaded detention room. . . .

Sydney H. Bass was a Methodist Episcopal minister who immigrated from England in 1910. Detained for two days on Ellis Island because of a crippled leg, Bass was appalled by conditions at the station, especially in the detention or "common" room, where detainees awaited special inquiry. And he particularly objected to being incarcerated with people of other nationalities whom he considered inferior to himself. Bass gave testimony six months later at House of Representatives investigative hearings.

I arrived at Ellis Island about 8:30 on the following morning, when I went in line, single file, with the other immigrants. I make no complaint about these things. I do not complain about the immigration law, and I always endeavor to carry out all the requirements of the law.

On arriving at Ellis Island the first thing that occurred that gave an indication of what I might expect was the porter putting us in line and calling out: 'Get on up stairs, you cattle. You will soon have a nice little pen.'

Then I went to the first inspector, and he said: 'Are you an American citizen?' I said: 'No, sir; British.' He said: 'What is your occupation?' I said: 'My profession is that of a minister of the Gospel.' He said: 'Right. Go in there,' and he put me in the first pen. . . . .

Then, of course, I had my medical examination, and I took my certificate, which showed that I had had infantile paralysis of the right leg. I explained to the doctor, facetiously, that I did not preach with my feet, and he said: 'All right. You can straighten that out with the immigration authorities.'

After going through the various pens, I arrived at 9:30 in the common room and that is the basis of the bulk of my complaint. . . . . There is awful congestion there, and it is the height of cruelty to herd people together in such crowded, congested quarters, under such unsanitary conditions, where there is not sufficient air space. . . . . I objected to being placed there in such close proximity with the

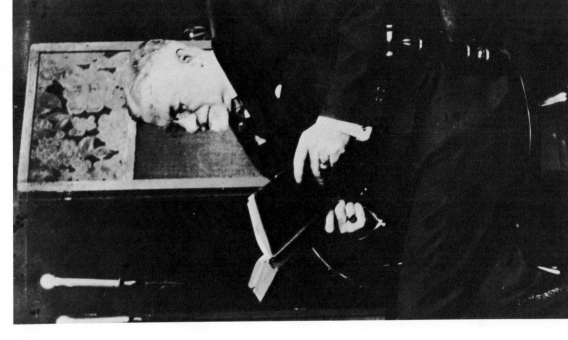

Opposite: Affected by economic depression and religious persecution, Russian Jews emigrated to America by the hundreds of thousands in the first decade of the century. Not just Russians, however, but Eastern European Jews in general viewed America as their goldene medine (golden land).

Fortunately for historians of Ellis Island, photography was rapidly growing as a profession at the turn of the century. Chief clerk Augustus Sherman, at left, was himself a hobbyist; many of his photographs of immigrants appear in this chapter.

Lewis Hine, one of the best social documentarians in the history of photography, did a study of immigrants at Ellis Island. Some of his subjects were: at right, a Russian Jewess; opposite, clockwise from top left, a Finnish stowaway, an Armenian Jew, a Russian woman with her children, an Italian child clutching a penny, a Syrian Arab, and an Albanian woman in native costume.

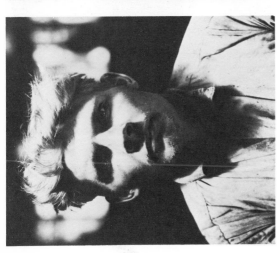

This colorful family of Magyar Gypsies was deported en masse in 1905.

filthiest people of all nations, covered with dirt and vermin, and while I did not take any dirt or vermin there, I can not guarantee that I did not take a considerable amount away with me from Ellis Island. . . .

I was there on the first day from 9:30 in the morning until 7:30 at night, standing all the time, except occasionally when I sat on the ground. I said to the inspector, 'It seems an anomaly to hold me up for a bad leg and then make me stand on it all those hours. . . .'

For three of the hours I was standing hemmed in on all four sides by Italian immigrants very much taller than I, I being short. They were eating garlic, and you can imagine how offensive it was. It was very unpleasant. It made it difficult for me to breathe. The smell was worse than I ever smelled before, and I have worked at my profession in slums of our large towns in England. You could almost taste and feel it, as well as smell it.

I then went before the board of special inquiry, and they seemed to give me apparently a very fair hearing. I spoke as I am speaking to you now, without interruption; but they refused to look at my conference credentials during the hearing, and at the conclusion of it I was unanimously ordered to be deported as an alien without visible means of support and as liable to become a public charge. Of course my means of support are invisible.

I asked permission to wire, as I have said, and they refused me. During all the time I was there not a single visitor came in the [common] room, but an Irishman was in charge who, in keeping order, knocked the im-

migrants on the head with a brush. A great deal goes on there that Commissioner Williams does not hear of and probably does not know about. . . .

Commissioner Williams also gave extensive testimony at these Congressional hearings. He admitted to various problems at the island but said he thought that Bass often exaggerated his experiences for dramatic effect. Although observers on other occasions corroborated parts of Bass's story, Williams defended his administration well at this hearing, and all charges were dropped.

Stephen Graham, another Britisher, also felt "dehumanized" when he was processed in 1913. His account was published the next year in *With Poor Immigrants to America*. Graham mentions the "place where marriages were solemnised," which was called the "Kissing Post." It was in a partitioned area behind the primary inspection desks where, as one former Ellis Island employee recalled, not only marriages took place but unions of all kinds in which "friends, sweethearts, husbands and wives, parents and children would greet one another, embrace and kiss and shed tears for pure joy."

The day of the emigrants' arrival in New York was the nearest earthly likeness to the final Day of Judgment, when we have to prove our fitness to enter Heaven. . . .

The hall of judgment [Registry] was crowned by two immense American flags. The centre, and indeed the great body of the hall, was filled with immigrants in their stalls, a long series of classified third-class men and women. The walls of the hall were booking-offices, bank counters, inspectors' tables, stools of statisticians. Up above was a visitors' gallery where journalists and the curious

might promenade and talk about the melting-pot, and America, 'the refuge of the oppressed.'

Somewhere also there was a place where marriages were solemnised. Engaged couples were there made man and wife before landing in New York. I was helping a girl who struggled with a huge basket, and a detective asked me if she were my sweetheart. If I could have said 'Yes,' as like as not we'd have been married off before we landed. America is extremely solicitous about the welfare of women, especially of poor unmarried women who come to her shores. So many women fall into the clutches of evil directly they land in the New World. The authorities generally refuse to admit a poor friendless girl, though there is a great demand for female labour all over the United States, and it is easy to get a place and earn an honest living. . . .

At three in the afternoon I stood in another ferry-boat, and with a crowd of approved immigrants passed the City of New York. Success had melted most of us, and though we were terribly hungry, we had words and confidences for one another on that ferry-boat. We were ready to help one another to any extent in our power. That is what it feels like to have passed the Last Day and still believe in Heaven, to pass Ellis Island and still believe in America.

Louis Adamic, a Slovenian immigrant who came through Ellis Island in 1913, told his story most eloquently almost twenty years later in *Laughing in the Jungle*.

I had written Stefan ('Steve') Radin, brother of my late friend Yanko, whose address in Brooklyn I happened to have, that I was due in New York on December 30th, and would he meet me on Ellis Island, which Peter Molek had told me was the clearing-house for immigrants?

The day I spent on Ellis Island was an eternity. Rumors were current among immigrants of several nationalities that some of us would be refused admittance into the United States and sent back to Europe. For several hours I was in a cold sweat on this account, although, so far as I knew, all my papers were in order, and sewed away in the lining of my jacket were twenty-five dollars in American currency—the minimum amount required by law to be in the possession of every immigrant before entering the country. Then, having rationalized away some of these fears, I gradually worked up a panicky feeling that I might develop measles or smallpox, or some other such disease. I heard that several hundred sick immigrants were quarantined on the island.

The first night in America I spent, with hundreds of other recently arrived immigrants, in an immense hall with tiers of narrow iron-and-canvas bunks, four deep. I was assigned a top bunk. Unlike most of the steerage immigrants, I had no bedding with me, and the blanket which someone threw at me was too thin to be effective against the blasts of cold air that rushed in through the open windows; so that I shivered, sleepless, all night, listening to snores and dream-monologues in perhaps a dozen different languages.

The bunk immediately beneath mine was occupied by a Turk, who slept with his turban wound around his head. He was tall, thin,

Some midgets, photographed in 1911, probably belonged to a troupe of entertainers. As such, they would have been admitted temporarily.

dark, bearded, hollow-faced, and hook-nosed. At peace with Allah, he snored all night, producing a thin wheezing sound, which occasionally, for a moment or two, took on a deeper note.

I thought how curious it was that I should be spending a night in such proximity to a Turk, for Turks were traditional enemies of Balkan peoples, including my own nation. For centuries Turks had forayed into Slovenian territory. Now here I was, trying to sleep directly above a Turk, with only a sheet of canvas between us. . . .

Late in the afternoon of the last day of 1913 I was examined for entry into the United States, with about a hundred other immigrants who had come on the *Niagara*. . . .

The official spoke a bewildering mixture of many Slavic languages. He had a stern voice and a sour visage. I had difficulty understanding some of his questions. . . .

Then the inspector waved me out of his presence and the clerk motioned me to go back and sit on one of the benches near by.

I waited another hour. It got dark and the lights were turned on in the room.

Finally, after dozens of other immigrants had been questioned, Steve Radin was called into the examining-room and asked, in English, to state his relationship to me.

He answered, of course, that he was not related to me at all.

Whereupon the inspector fairly pounced upon me, speaking the dreadful botch of Slavic languages. What did I mean by lying to him? He said a great many other things which I did not understand. I did comprehend,

however, his threat to return me to the Old Country. It appeared that America had no room for liars: America was glad to welcome to its shores only decent, honest, truthful people.

My heart pounded.

Finally it occurred simultaneously to me and to Steve Radin that the man must be laboring under some misapprehension. And, truly, before another minute elapsed it turned out that the clerk had made a mistake by entering on my paper that I had declared Stefan Radin was my uncle. How the mistake occurred I do not know; perhaps the clerk had confused my questionnaire form with some one else's.

Finally, perceiving the error, the examiner's face formed in a grimace and, waving his hand in a casual gesture, he ordered me released. . . .

Steve Radin picked up my bag and, in the confusion, I barely remembered to say goodby to Peter Molek, who was going to Pennsylvania.

I was weak in the knees and just managed to walk out of the room, then downstairs and onto the ferryboat. I had been shouted at, denounced as a liar by an official of the United States in my second day in the country, before a roomful of people, including Steve Radin, whom, so far, I had merely glimpsed.

But the weakness in my knees soon passed. I laughed, perhaps a bit hysterically, as the little Ellis Island ferryboat bounded over the rough, white-capped waters of the bay toward the Battery.

Steve Radin gaped at me. Then he smiled.

I was in New York—in America.

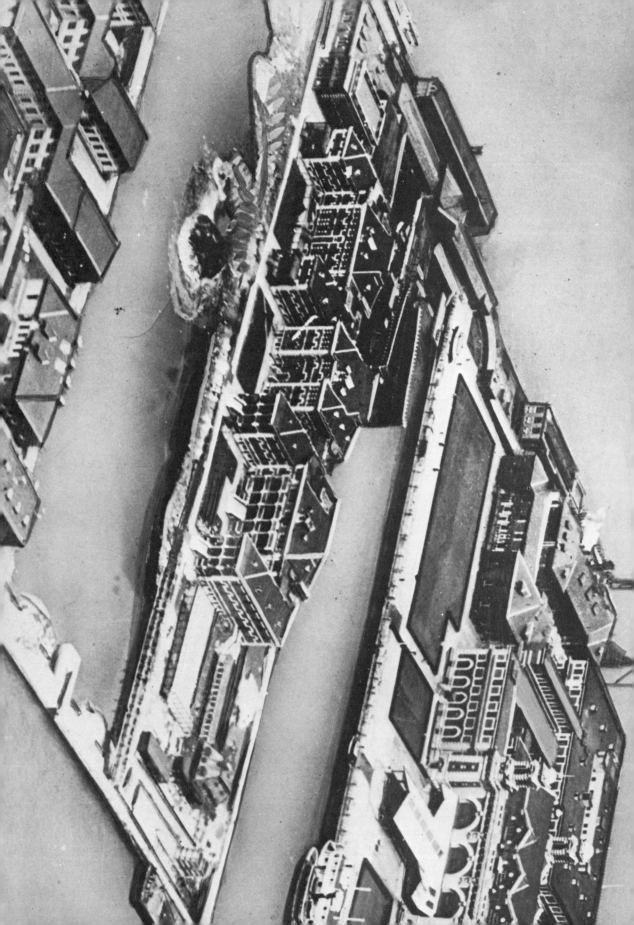

CHAPTER FIVE
DECLINE

JULIAN KAISER

The quota laws of 1921 and 1924, limiting the numbers of immigrants by a "national origins" formula, cut the annual immigration figures to a fraction of what they had been before World War I. As immigration declined, so did the station's use as a receiving depot. By the 1930s Ellis Island was principally a detention and deportation center.

The aerial photograph at left, taken on a snowy day in the early 1920s, shows the island virtually deserted. Arrivals were always fewest in the winter months. A single barge and the Ellis Island tugboat are docked at the slip.

NATIONAL ARCHIVES

The outbreak of World War I in August 1914 caused an immediate reduction in immigration. That year the total number of arrivals at Ellis Island was 878,052; the following year the number dropped nearly eighty percent to 178,416; by 1918, the last year of the war, it was down to 28,867. Because there were drastically fewer immigrants to process, the Ellis Island work force was also reduced. By the end of the war, almost half of the staff—including inspectors, interpreters, clerks, and watchmen—had been dismissed or sent on indefinite furlough. Most did not return to the force after the war, and the administrative process, so painstakingly evolved under Commissioners Williams and Watchorn, never again achieved its prewar efficiency.

A more positive effect of the decrease in immigration was the opportunity for the Medical Division, which did not suffer a reduction of staff, to give more intensive physical and mental examinations. Not surprisingly, the result was that a greater number of medical certifications led to special inquiry (3.26 percent of arrivals in 1915, as compared to 2.29 percent in 1914). In addition, the hospitals on Islands 2 and 3 were devoted to intensive medical research programs. Bacteriologists in the Public Health Service conducted laboratory experiments on trachoma and on parasitic and venereal diseases. They also developed new procedures for diagnosing and preventing the spread of communicable diseases within the hospitals.

Commissioner Williams resigned his second term in 1913. He was temporarily replaced by Acting Commissioner Byron Uhl. About a year later, a month after the outbreak of war, President Woodrow Wilson appointed one of his former graduate students at Princeton, Frederic C. Howe, to the post. Howe was a well-known municipal reformer who had most recently been director of the People's Institute at Cooper Union, a university in New York City. Howe came to office determined to

"humanize" Ellis Island and to change its reputation as the "Island of Tears." During his first year on the island, he put into effect a number of measures that helped make life a little less grim for detainees.

Commissioner Howe allowed women and children, who had previously been kept indoors, use of the lawns as play areas most of the day as long as weather permitted. He converted one of the large balconies into a meeting area where men and women could be together at times during the day other than meals. Realizing that many of the women held on suspicion of prostitution were actually innocent, he allowed them to roam as freely as other detainees. He arranged concerts, motion pictures, holiday celebrations, classes for women and children in sewing and knitting, a kindergarten for younger children, and organized athletics for men. He recruited teachers from New York City to give instruction in English, hygiene, child care, and other elementary subjects and attempted to beautify the station, particularly the Registry, with flags, plants, and scenic pictures of the United States. Howe placed complaint and suggestion boxes around the station and encouraged employees to form a union-like organization. His first winter in office, he gave shelter, too, to some 750 homeless men from New York, providing beds and breakfast and ferry service back to Manhattan each morning so they could look for work. Many years later, Howe recorded in his autobiography, *Confessions of a Reformer:*

For over a year things went well on the island. The newspapers gave space to the new ideas that I had introduced, the attempt to care for the thousands of aliens who, as a result of war, found themselves without a country, wards of the United States government. I spoke before chambers of commerce, clubs, colleges, and universities. I took an active part in the movement to Americanize the alien, especially in trying to interpret his wants, as opposed to the wants which his self-constituted guardians thought he ought to have.

It was true that at first the public and press were warmly supportive of Howe's reforms on Ellis Island, but it was only a matter of a short time before his liberal activities attracted criticism from various business and political interests. His recommendation that second-class cabin passengers be inspected on Ellis Island, where their dealings with hotel keepers, restaurateurs, bankers, and transportation companies could be overseen by government officials, offended many businessmen who would have been deprived of profits. His requests that the rates charged steamship companies for hospitalization of sick aliens be raised and that the food concession be cancelled in favor of a government-run restaurant brought additional storms of protest. Congressman William Bennett of New York—who happened to be the lawyer for the food contractor—led the attack, calling Howe "a half-baked radical" with "free-love ideas." Howe ably defended his policies in letters to his superiors in Washington and to the press, but was unable to clear himself entirely of the growing suspicion that he was a dangerous sort of innovator.

Howe's controversy with Bennett was interrupted by the worst physical disaster on Ellis Island since the burning of the original station in 1897 (see Chapter 2, page 39). Early in the morning of July 30, 1916, German saboteurs set fire to wharves on the Black Tom River in New Jersey, less than a mile away, where munitions were stacked on barges in readiness for shipment to Russia. Seven warehouses at the wharves went up in flames, detonating the munitions. The blasts went on for several hours, shattering plate glass as far away as Times Square. On Ellis Island all windows and doors on Islands 1 and 2 were blown in and several small fires were started by the shower of burning debris.

Frederic Theis, an assistant superintendent at the Ellis Island hospital, told his version of events some years later to then-commissioner Edward Corsi, who recorded the account in his autobiography, *In the Shadow of Liberty*. Theis looked out the hospital window toward New Jersey and saw

...an inferno pierced by deafening explosions and the detonation of shells.

The tide was coming in, and a west wind carried the fire toward the barges moored at the Black Tom Wharves. Suddenly I saw that the barges, which had been moored by the usual hemp rope, had caught fire and were exploding as they drifted toward Ellis Island. Already the Ellis Island windows had been broken, the doors had been jammed inward, and parts of the roofs had collapsed.

Acting in conjunction with my associates, I hastened to assist in the removal of our insane patients to the tennis courts. We wrapped them in blankets and carried them out into the open air.

When we had them out of doors, they presented one of the most extraordinary spectacles I have ever seen. As the five-inch shells flared over the Island like skyrockets, the poor demented creatures clapped their hands and cheered, laughed and sang and cried, thinking it was a show which had been arranged for their particular amusement....

We thought for a time that the final explosion had occurred. Then we learned that the barges which had floated against the Island and set fire to the sea wall were loaded with munitions. It was then that we who had to care

Right, morgue and autopsy room, summer 1983; opposite, hospital laboratory, about 1916

JULIAN KAISER

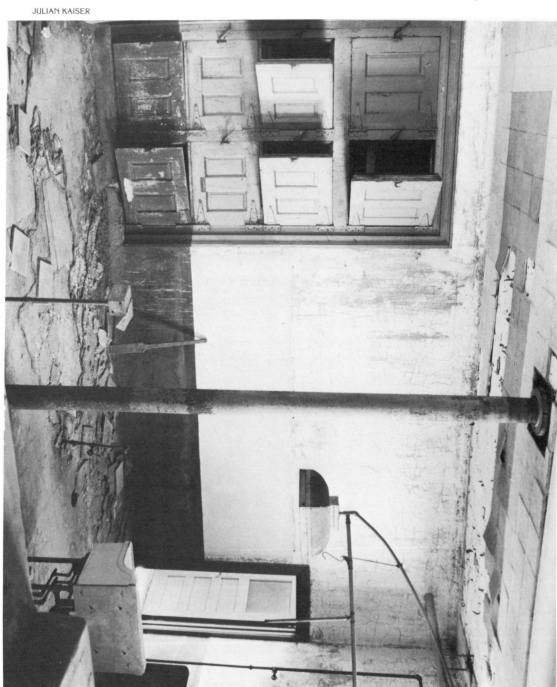

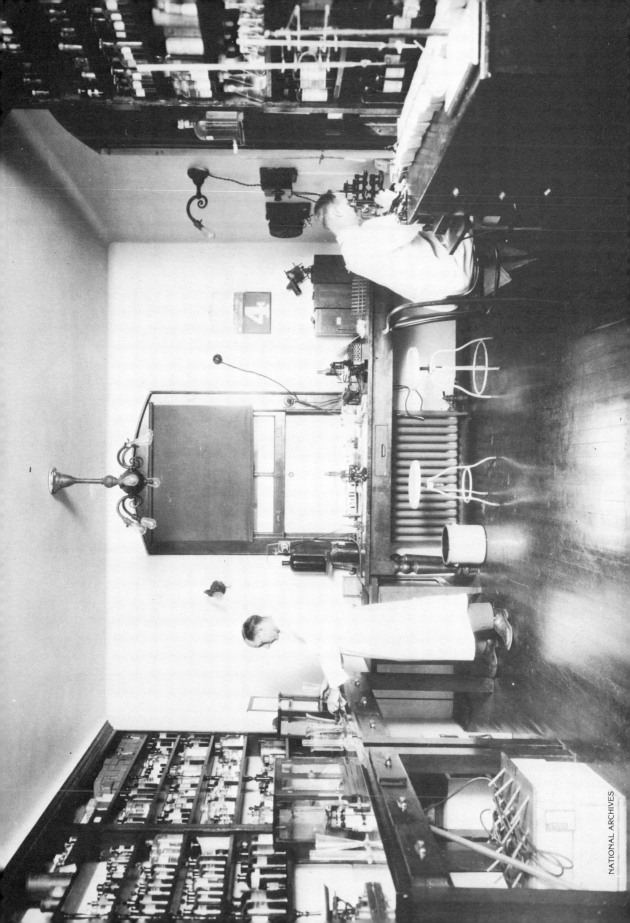

for the patients first realized to what extent our own lives were in danger. Fortunately the heroism of those who manned the tugs of the Lehigh Valley Railroad saved us. They towed the two flaming barges out to sea, where they sank amid concussions which sounded like the end of the world. . . .

We bivouacked on the tennis court for the rest of the night, vainly trying to pacify the insane who were disappointed that the show was over. At 7:00 AM we cleaned up and returned the patients to the hospital. . . .

Most of the 600 people on Ellis at the time were evacuated to the Battery. Miraculously, no one on the island was seriously hurt—only Chief Clerk August Sherman's office cat, which was cut by flying glass.

Property damage—estimated at $400,000—was another matter. The New York Times reported the next day that the grounds were covered with broken glass, charred wood, cinders, and all kinds of debris. The great arched windows and doors of the main building were blown in "as if with a charge of dynamite." The ceiling in the Registry collapsed. The dining room, the executive offices, and the board room were wrecked. In the Contagious Disease Hospital, the five bathrooms were turned inside out. Taps were wrenched off, pipes twisted like pieces of paper, and tubs turned completely over. It was as if Ellis Island had been the scene of a battle.

Less than a year later, even as repairs were being made on the island, the United States entered the "Great War." Immediately, 1,170 officers and crewmen of German and Austrian ships harbored in New York and New London were seized and transferred to Ellis for internment. This emergency called for a complete rearrangement of quarters, the shifting of detained immigrants to other rooms, and the reorganization of the administration. The entire Baggage and Dormitory Building was given over to the crewmen and to a detachment of soldiers detailed by the War Department to guard them. With sentries, stockades, and floodlights, Ellis Island began to look more like a prison camp than an immigration depot, but the prisoners were treated well. Despite their petitions and complaints about bad food and drafty quarters, their chief discomfort, according to The New York Times, was "boredom and the lack of beer."

Their presence on the island, however, along with that of several other classes of detainees—German immigrants, suspected spies, etc.—placed a strain on the reduced work force. In his annual report to the Commissioner General of Immigration, Howe complained that in some instances the detainees were

. . . very difficult to control. The task of seeing to it that they did not escape and conducted no correspondence or interviews except in accord with the limitations necessary by reason of their status added much to the duties and anxiety of the officers here. They were inspected twice daily by medical officers; it was necessary carefully to examine all packages received for them, and to obtain proper clothing and other necessaries for those who had been arrested and delivered to us with practically no personal effects.

The national hysteria over the "Hun" in America created intense pressure for Commissioner Howe, who felt he had to be constantly at war with his own staff to ensure good treatment of the German detainees and with an army of Secret Service agents to prevent needless internment of innocent people. He was quickly branded pro-German.

Just two months before the United States entered the war, an important immigration law had been passed. Based on the recommendations of a commission created ten years earlier to study the immigration issue, the new law codified thirty-three different classes of aliens to be excluded from the United States. One important new category was the illiterate—anyone over the age of sixteen who could not read at least forty simple words of some language was debarred. Political and religious refugees were exempt, as were the wives and elderly relatives of aliens already admitted. The law also excluded all Asiatics not already encompassed by the Chinese exclusion laws and the "gentlemen's agreement" with Japan (in which, in exchange for certain trade privileges, Japan would not allow its citizens to emigrate) and created, by degrees of latitude and longitude, a "barred zone" that eliminated immigrants from most Middle Eastern, Far Eastern, and Southern Pacific countries.

Opponents of the literacy requirement (including President Wilson, whose veto of the law was overridden) objected on the grounds that it discriminated against people who had not had educational opportunities, regardless of other attributes in their favor. Nevertheless, the new law would remain basic to American immigration policy for the next thirty-five years.

In 1918 Ellis Island was given over to the war effort. Most of the 2,200 foreign crewmen and people of "suspected loyalty" detained on the island were transferred to detention camps in North Carolina and Georgia so that the island could be made available to the armed forces. Regular inspection of arriving aliens was done on board ship or at the docks.

The navy took over the Baggage and Dormitory Building and the area previously used as the railroad ticket office and waiting rooms. These quarters housed seamen awaiting ship assignments. The army took over the Registry and special inquiry rooms and all twenty-one hospital buildings. These were used for returning soldiers whose illnesses and wounds demanded immediate care when they were removed from transports in New York. When able to move, these patients were transferred to mainland hospitals. The Immigration Service retained only minimum area for aliens held for special inquiry and those waiting to be released to relatives, but it continued to administer the entire station, supplying heat, electricity, telephone service, and building maintenance.

The first 100 wounded doughboys—amputees and victims of shell shock—arrived in March 1918. One immigration official later remembered that it was terrible to see young men so wounded. By early 1919 the hospital had 1,100 beds, with a rapid turnover of patients. The largest ward at Ellis—indeed, in the country —was the Registry, or Ward 34, which could handle 260 ambulatory, medical, psychopathic, and surgical patients. The advantages of using Ellis Island for military hospitalization, according to *The New York Times*, included "the benefit of sea air on the recovery of the men, and the advantage of keeping them away from the temptations and excitement to which they would be subjected in cities and hospitals near army camps." The disadvantage, of course, was that there was not much on the island in the way of recreation. Convalescent soldiers were as bored on Ellis as detained aliens had been.

In the summer of 1919, the navy and army returned Ellis Island to the Immigration Service. In most cases the buildings were in as good as or better condition than they had been before the war. (The army had constructed a covered walkway between Islands 1 and 2

Right, operating room, about 1916;
opposite, Red Cross reading room
adjacent to Registry ward, about
1916

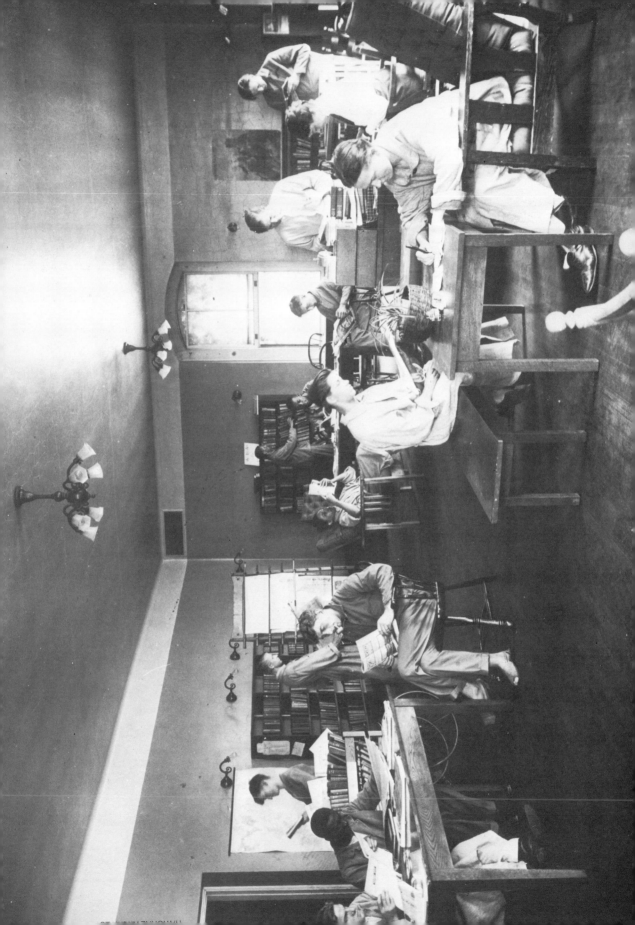

and installed dental facilities in the hospital.) In short time the island was ready again to receive what was anticipated to be a new surge of European immigration.

Toward the end of the war, even while the armed forces were using most of the buildings, a growing number of aliens were detained on Ellis by the Justice Department on suspicion of being Communists or Communist sympathizers. In fact, the national fear of the "Hun" was gradually being replaced by a fear of the "Red."

In 1918 a new law was passed that made it easier to deport "anarchists and persons advocating the overthrow of the government by force or violence." This included anyone who belonged to an organization advocating revolt or who wrote or published or even possessed anarchist literature. The law stipulated that such deportees could never reenter the United States and made it a felony for them to attempt to do so.

According to Commissioner Howe, at this time the administration of Ellis Island "was confused by byproducts of the war. For two years, instead of being the commissioner of immigration, he became a jailer ". . . not of convicted offenders but of suspected persons who had been arrested and railroaded to Ellis Island as the most available dumping-ground under the successive waves of hysteria which swept the country."

The first trainload of "Reds," a group of fifty-four "Wobblies" (members of the Industrial Workers of the World) from the lumber camps of Washington State, arrived while Howe was attending the peace conference in Paris. The press dubbed the train "the Red Special" and widely assumed that its passengers would be quickly deported. Under orders from Washington, Acting Commissioner Uhl held the Wobblies incommunicado and, at first, without legal representation. After his return a month later, an infuriated Howe refused to rush the men into deportation, and his pro-

tests were instrumental in getting them further hearings.

A second group of 200 "Reds" were soon arrested by the New York City police bomb squad in a raid on the headquarters of the Union of Russian Peasant Workers of America. Most of these recently arrived "undesirables" were quickly released; three, "who believed absolutely in force and violence," were imprisoned on Ellis.

Soon a backlash from the press and the more liberal elements of government caused the Department of Justice to curtail these hasty and arbitrary mass arrests, and Howe resumed his place on the peace delegation in Paris. When he returned to Ellis Island that summer, however, he found himself accused of being pro-Communist. Later that fall, besieged with demands for his resignation, he bitterly obliged his detractors. In hearings conducted on Ellis by the House Committee on Immigration and Naturalization after his resignation (and temporary replacement, once again, by Byron Uhl), the ex-commissioner was blamed for the fact that only sixty of the 697 anarchists detained on Ellis to date had actually been deported. He was accused of consorting with the anarchists, of tolerating immorality and gambling on the island, and of allowing the "preaching of Bolshevism and the circulation of Red literature." When Howe demanded his right to testify in his own behalf and to cross-examine witnesses, he was ejected from the hearings. Years later he wrote in his autobiography:

As I look back over these years, my outstanding memories are not of the immigrant. They are rather of my own people. Things that were done forced one almost to despair of the mind, to distrust the political state. Shreds were left of our courage, our reverence. The

Department of Justice, the Department of Labor, and Congress not only failed to protest against hysteria, they encouraged these excesses; the state not only abandoned the liberty which it should have protected, it lent itself to the stamping out of individualism and freedom. It used the agent provocateur, it permitted private agencies to usurp government powers, turned over the administration of justice to detective agencies, card-indexed liberals and progressives. It became frankly an agency of employment and business interests at a time when humanity—the masses, the poor—were making the supreme sacrifice of their lives. . . . .

Soon there was another brief flurry of mass arrests of alien radicals, and Acting Commissioner Uhl cooperated with the Justice Department in their speedy deportation. Certainly one of the most notorious events of the Red Scare period at Ellis was the unannounced sailing of the army transport *Buford* in the middle of a bitter winter's night in late 1919, carrying 249 deportees to Russia, including the famous anarchist Emma Goldman. In fact, the mass deportation had been rumored for some time, but as Goldman recounted, the actual hour of departure came as a surprise:

On the night we were taken away I was writing a pamphlet on deportation at 2:00 A.M. I did not dream that we would be going for several days. In fact, I had spoken with Superintendent Baker and others, telling them that we would like to know a day or two before our deportations in order that we might send for our clothes and personal belongings. You see —many of us had been jerked up wherever we were found, and not

permitted to communicate in any manner with our relatives until after we reached the Island.

Many of the poor working men were taken in their work clothes without so much as a chance to get changes of underwear, and not even at the last were they permitted to remove their savings from savings banks. I believe the savings of the entire lot amounted to something like sixty thousand dollars.

As I said, I was writing the pamphlet when a rap sounded on my door. It was one of the coldest nights of the year. I hurriedly hid the manuscript I was working upon and went•to the door.

An official said: 'Get your things together— you're being taken to the deportation boat!'

Those who were sleeping were pulled from their beds. We were marched between two long lines of soldiers with loaded guns to the cutter. We had to stand in the freezing cold. When two hours had elapsed we reached the *Buford.* Two hours later we were heading out to sea, and none of us knew where we were being taken.

Arrests in 1919 had exceeded 5,000, with nearly 3,000 held in detention around the country. About 500 of these were detained on Ellis. These, together with increasing immigrant arrivals, taxed the staff and facilities. Early in 1920, however, as a result of protests by many church, social, and legal organizations and the responsible action of some Labor Department officials, the Red Scare began to wane. Arrests fell off, and by midyear there were only about twenty-five so-called anarchists detained at Ellis. The staff was able once again to focus its attention on immigration.

After the war there was an immediate, noticeable increase in immigration—from 26,731 in 1919 to 225,206 in 1920. The number then more than doubled to 560,971 in 1921. Clearly, the new literacy test was not in itself enough to achieve the desired effect. The work force was increased but did not operate as efficiently as it had before the war. Furthermore, the more-detailed examination prescribed by the 1917 law, including the literacy test, slowed down processing to just 2,000 immigrants a day (as compared to the prewar rate of 5,000) and resulted in more detentions. Once again, shiploads of immigrants sometimes had to wait in the harbor until there was room for them on the island, and the press began to complain.

A new commissioner at Ellis, Frederick Wallis, replaced Uhl in 1920. Like his predecessors Wallis entered office with idealistic plans for improving conditions at the immigration station. Unfortunately, though able in many respects, he was not up to it and was soon complaining publicly about the overwhelming difficulties of the job. Much publicity, for example, was given to the problem of vermin and the resulting spread of typhus after the war. Conditions at Ellis Island, it was believed—and Wallis vociferously agreed —were a menace to the public health.

An ever-growing movement to reduce immigration picked up momentum, and in 1920 Congress voted to suspend all immigration for one year while it studied the problem and reformulated policy. The result was the passage in 1921 of a radically new type of legislation, the first "quota law." This law, a stopgap measure at first vetoed by Woodrow Wilson but later signed by Warren G. Harding, limited the number of immigrants of any one nationality entering the United States to three percent of foreign-born persons of that nationality living here in 1910, as determined by the census. The

total number of annual arrivals was not to exceed 357,803. Not more than twenty percent of the annual quota for any nationality could be landed monthly. This law ensured that the "new immigration" from southern and eastern Europe would be drastically reduced from its prewar level, while the "old immigration" from northern and western Europe would not be affected. Its impact was immediate. The number of arrivals at Ellis Island dropped to 209,778 in 1922 (the nationwide drop was from 805,228 in 1921 to 309,556 in 1922). The new policy was so successful that as soon as the law expired in 1922 it was extended to 1924.

On a more personal level the law had tragic results. With no limitations imposed at their ports of origin, steamship companies raced madly against each other to land as many immigrants as possible before the monthly quotas were filled. Consequently, hundreds of otherwise admissible people—who had disposed of their homes and other possessions to start a new life in America—were turned away. The staff at Ellis Island, far from inured to spectacles of misery, was subjected to entire boatloads of hysterical people. A physician, interviewed by *Literary Digest*, described the reaction of a group of 500 southeastern Europeans:

The ensuing demonstration of these excitable people is one of my most painful reminiscences of service at the Island. They screamed and bawled and beat about like wild animals, breaking the waiting room furniture and attacking the attendants, several of whom were severely hurt. It was a pitiful spectacle, but officials were helpless to aid.

After an unsuccessful attempt to persuade his superiors in Washington to institute a screening process in the ports of origin, Commissioner Wallis resigned in a state of disillusionment. His successor,

Robert Tod, reputedly an able administrator, was greeted enthusiastically by the press. He did implement numerous changes recommended by a committee appointed by the Department of Labor to study welfare work on Ellis Island, improving the services offered to immigrants immediately upon landing, rather than only after admission.

But conditions overall on Ellis did not improve substantially under Tod's administration, and with relief he returned to private business in 1923. His chief complaint about this job had been the unrelenting political pressure to make exceptions to the immigration laws and admit aliens who ought to have been excluded.

The next commissioner was another appointee of President Harding, Henry Curran, who knew well that he was "walking into a furnace." As principled as any of his predecessors, he continued the harangue with Washington over conditions at Ellis. His special complaint was about the detention policy, particularly the long delay in appeals against exclusion. He later wrote that the "shuttle service of papers, between Ellis Island and Washington made for delay, while the immigrants waited at the island, in an agony of suspense by day, in the wire cages by night. In hot weather their locked-up life on my island was a horror."

Meanwhile, barely noticed, a subtle but basic change in oceanic transportation had evolved. After the passage of literacy and quota requirements, the steamship companies discovered that steerage-class accommodations were no longer profitable and accordingly built their new liners with comfortable third-class cabins. In short time the misery of steerage, which undoubtedly had caused more torment than the worst conditions at Ellis, was a thing of the past.

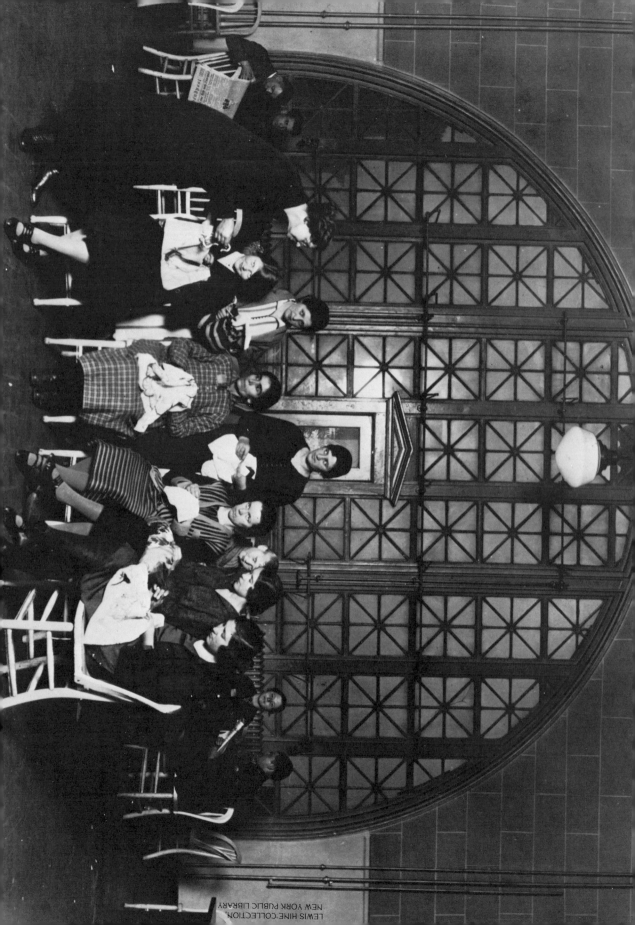

Opposite, Daughters of the American Revolution, one of several civic organizations that were involved in social work at Ellis Island, give instruction in sewing and needlework.

Left, arched window, Registry Room, spring 1985

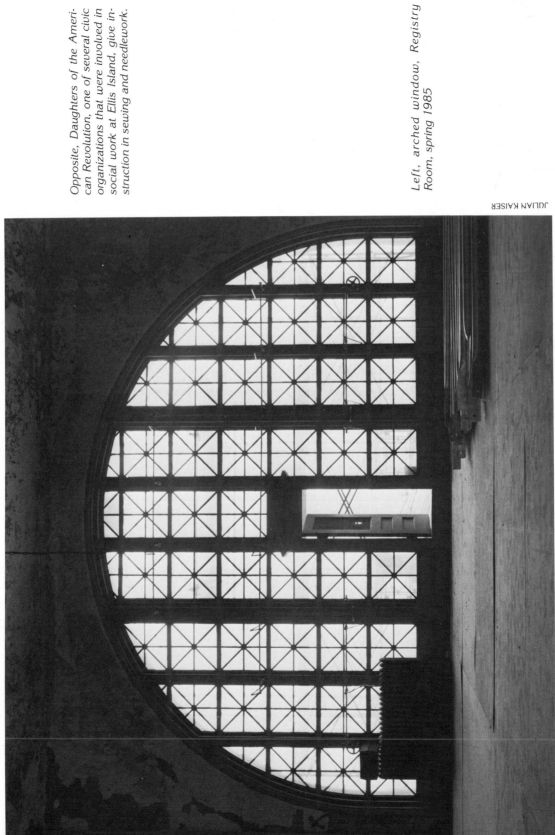

The group of gentlemen opposite, at least some of whom apparently are musicians, are being served refreshments by Ellis Island attendants. After World War I first- and second-class passengers from German ports frequently were detained for special inquiry.

The new laws seemed most effective in reducing the number of arrivals at official ports of entry in the United States, although officials were quick to note that immigrants, discouraged to go the official routes, were entering illegally in much greater numbers than previously through soft spots along the Mexican and Canadian borders. Lawmakers determined to place even stricter limitations on immigration passed a new quota law in 1924. This law reduced the quotas to two percent of the resident population of a nationality as of the 1890 census, and the annual total to 164,677. No more than ten percent of an annual quota could be admitted in one month. This new formula was even more weighted in favor of northern and western Europeans than the 1921 law. All immigrants were required to have visas issued by a United States consulate before they could be admitted, for the first time providing a method of selection and qualification in the countries of origin. In addition, they were to have health certificates supplied by local medical sources.

Congress and the Department of Labor congratulated themselves on the new "law with a heart." Gone was the congestion and most of the frustration at Ellis Island. The Immigration Service launched a long-overdue cleanup and refurbishing of the immigration station, but the fact was that this effort was almost past usefulness. The outdated, oversized, and now under-utilized complex of buildings was becoming a white elephant and very expensive to maintain.

The stock market crash of 1929 and the Great Depression that followed had a tremendous impact on immigration as well—so much so that it is difficult to evaluate the impact of the new legislation. By 1932 there were more people voluntarily leaving the country than trying to enter. Also, inspired by President Hoover, who wanted the borders closed, a new Secre-tary of Labor, William Doak, initiated yet another roundup of undesirables. Doak was of the opinion that there were at least 400,000 illegal aliens in America, and he set out to apprehend as many of them as possible. In short time he had deported nearly 1,000 people through Ellis Island.

In this atmosphere Edward Corsi—who had come through Ellis Island as a boy and done much social service work with immigrants as an adult—became commissioner of immigration. Corsi's greatest value as an administrator was his talent in public relations. He first set out to make life easier for detainees by liberalizing restrictions. He eased the rules and met with the men and women personally to hear grievances and work out problems. He also met with the local press, foreign-language correspondents, and the consuls of foreign nations in New York City and worked to improve relations between the bureau and department officials in Washington. After a visit with Corsi on Ellis Island, Secretary Doak was less inclined toward wholesale arrests. Corsi's influence was far-reaching—on his recommendation the administration of Franklin D. Roosevelt would appropriate more than $1.1 million from various public works funds for improvements at Ellis Island. He was not, however, able to prevent worker layoffs as a result of the Depression; the effectiveness of the staff was badly impaired by this necessity.

Corsi was succeeded by Rudolf Riemer, who oversaw Work Progress Administration projects initiated by his predecessor. From 1934 to 1937, in addition to major repairs to all the buildings, a new seawall and landfill between Islands 2 and 3, a fireproof brick ferry house, a central pavilion to house the Customs Service, and a new kitchen, a greenhouse, an immigrant building (as

WPA projects of the 1930s, including a new ferry building (opposite) and recreation building (right), were among the last improvements on Ellis Island.

NATIONAL ARCHIVES

distinct from the old buildings that housed only alien detainees), and a recreation building and shelters were all completed. The noted artist Edward Laning was commissioned to paint an 800-square-foot mural depicting the role of the immigrant in American industry. This was completed and mounted in the dining room in 1938. The WPA effort was the last significant construction on Ellis Island. Ironically, the funds for the improved facilities were available long after the greatest need for them had passed.

Early in the decade yet another scandal involving Ellis Island employees broke in the press. This time it involved the sale of fraudulent citizenship papers, discovered when the Immigration and Naturalization Services were being consolidated. The investigation, which went on for a decade, resulted in the successful prosecution of over 250 racketeers, island employees, aliens, and steamship companies. Ultimately, the inquiry focused on many illegal activities, including registry frauds, visa frauds, the smuggling of aliens,

NATIONAL ARCHIVES

NATIONAL PARK SERVICE

and seamen's certificate frauds.

Late in the 1930s, with the rise of Nazism in Germany and then in Austria, pressure was exerted to relax immigration policy in favor of refugees from persecution, especially Jews, but restrictionists in Congress, staunchly backed by labor unions, would not yield, and the Roosevelt administration failed to overcome the bloc. The total number of refugees from Nazism who were allowed into the United States was no more than 250,000.

With the outbreak of World War II the Coast Guard moved into Ellis Island, making it a training station and a site from which to conduct coastal patrols to enforce the Neutrality Act. Over a period of seven years, some 63,000 guardsmen were trained on Ellis Island, then shipped out to naval fronts all over the world.

In the late 1940s, when most immigrants were admitted under the Displaced Person's Act, the Registry (left) became a recreation hall. The cartoon below voices President Truman's irritation with an increasingly conservative immigration policy, while the cartoon at right reflects the concern of organized labor about unrestricted immigration.

"What Happened To The One We Used To Have?"

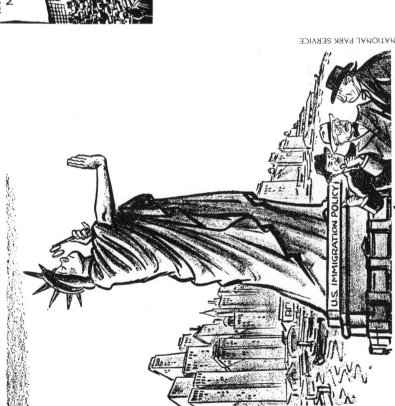

NATIONAL PARK SERVICE

Detention in the 1950s: Opposite, the men's exercise yard; far left, a hearing; left, detainees being escorted to Ellis.

Overleaf: Recreation building—at left, summer 1984; at right, shortly after its completion in 1937

As in World War I, enemy aliens who could not be returned to their home countries were detained at Ellis and other holding pens for the duration of the conflict. The Immigration and Naturalization Service was temporarily transferred to Manhattan.

Immigration legislation during the war reflected the growing concern over national security. In 1940 the Im-migration and Naturalization Service was subsumed under the Department of Justice. Laws were passed that required all aliens entering the country or already in it to be fingerprinted. (One exception to the prevailing mood was the repeal in 1943 of the Chinese exclusion acts dating back to 1882. A quota of 105 was assigned to Chinese aliens.)

After the war the Coast Guard quickly decommissioned Ellis Island, and the Immigration Service moved back. Under the influence of President Harry Truman and other liberals, Congress passed the War Brides Act, which admitted the wives of American servicemen, and the Displaced Persons' Act, which authorized quota visas to refugees in the French, British, and American zones in Germany, Italy, and Austria. From 1948 to 1952 nearly 400,000 immigrants were admitted under the provisions of this far-reaching legislation.

Then in 1950, in an atmosphere created by the Cold War and the Korean conflict, the Internal Security Act made membership in or adherence to the beliefs of Communist or totalitarian organizations cause for exclusion or denial of naturalization. The law also made a speaking knowledge of English mandatory for naturalization. Passed over the veto of President Truman, this law caused much anguish at Ellis Island, where refugees who had joined totalitarian organizations in order to eat during the war were being denied admission. Mercifully, a year later the law was amended to forgive such "nominal memberships."

The Immigration and Naturalization Act of 1952, also known as the McCarran-Walter Act, another piece of legislation passed over President Truman's veto, was based on a five-year study by the Justice Department. Its purpose was to repeal all immigration and naturalization laws on the books and to enact a completely revised policy. Essentially, it retained the national origins plan and quota systems, which it made even more rigidly repressive, and also provided for more thorough screening of aliens and broadened the grounds for exclusion and deportation of criminal aliens. But it also eliminated racial and sexual discrimination and introduced a special preference list of skilled aliens urgently needed in the country.

JULIAN KAISER

Left, Island 3, summer 1983; above, main building dormitory room, summer 1984; right, main building social services area, summer 1983

ELIZABETH GLASGOW

Left, laundry, spring 1985; above, incinerators, summer 1983; right, powerhouse, summer 1983

Overleaf: Baggage and Dormitory Building, summer 1983

Despite its more restrictive elements, the McCarran-Walter Act marked the beginning of an era of a more relaxed immigration policy. Within a year several amendments and the Refugee Relief Act made exceptions to the quotas in favor of distressed peoples in overpopulated countries and those fleeing from behind the Iron Curtain.

In the early 1950s Ellis Island gradually quieted down, with rarely more than a few hundred detainees on the island at any time. Once again maintenance of the vast, unused buildings became an expensive problem. The administrative offices of the Immigration and Naturalization Service, it was thought, could easily be permanently moved to a government office building in Manhattan, but the housing of detainees remained a problem. This was solved simply with a humanitarian ruling announced in November 1954 by the Attorney General at naturalization ceremonies for 16,000 people held at Ebbets Field and the Polo Grounds in Brooklyn. Thereafter, except for "those regarded as likely to abscond, or who might be risks to national security or public safety," there would be no more detainees. Aliens with purely technical difficulties would be released on conditional parole or bond.

Within ten days the population of detained aliens on Ellis Island was down to about twenty-five, and on November 29, 1954, when the ferryboat *Ellis Island* made its last run to the Battery and back, the island was vacant. The last detainee was Arne Petersen, a Norwegian seaman who had jumped ship and was held only three days before he was returned on parole to his country. *The New York Times* noted that six guards "charged with making round-the-clock patrols" would be the "only human population" on the island that had borne the footsteps of millions.

JULIAN KAISER

CHAPTER SIX
RESTORATION

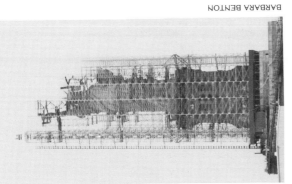

BARBARA BENTON

An extensive restoration program for both the Statue of Liberty and Ellis Island began in 1982. Scaffolding veiled the statue (far left and above) for nearly three years while it was cleaned and restored for its centennial in 1986. Other improvements include the installation of a glass-walled hydraulic elevator, allowing visitors to observe the details of the interior, and a new museum. Restoration of Ellis Island (left) is proceeding more slowly, to be concluded by its centennial in 1992.

JULIAN KAISER

RESTORATION   167

Street light, Island 2, near the recreation shelter, summer 1982

After its closing in November 1954, Ellis Island was turned over to the General Services Administration (GSA), whose business it is to administer United States property. The GSA first canvassed federal agencies to see if the island could be used for other governmental purposes. As there were no immediate ideas, the GSA declared Ellis Island to be "excess federal property" and began to consider proposals from state and local agencies and from nonprofit institutions: New York City wanted the island for a home for the aged, the homeless, or for delinquent boys. New York State wanted it for several possible uses, including an alcoholic clinic. New Jersey officials reopened the old debate with New York about boundary lines in an attempt to include Ellis Island in plans for a shoreline park. A group of importers and exporters wanted it for an international trade center.

However, the GSA was required by law to obtain fifty percent of the fair market value of the island, judged to be $6.3 million, based on original construction costs and improvements over fifty years. This figure—plus the costs of renovation, maintenance, and operation of the ferry—was enough to deter even the most hopeful agencies.

The GSA next attempted to sell Ellis Island for private commercial use. Although about twenty companies requested inspection tours of the island with a view to putting in bids, most of them were discouraged by the same financial considerations. The highest bid—less than a quarter million dollars by a real estate developer who intended to create a resort called "Pleasure Island"—was rejected by the GSA.

Meanwhile, the Ellis Island buildings began to succumb to the inevitable effects of weathering and lack of upkeep. In 1958 a reporter for The New Yorker described the island, minimally maintained by a staff of ten, as "very dilapidated." In dusty rooms barely

JULIAN KAISER

heated and dimly lit, fixtures rusted and paint peeled off the walls, while increasingly, at night, thieves hauled away furniture, copper piping, and anything else of value.

In 1959 and 1960 the GSA attempted, again unsuccessfully, to sell the island to the highest bidder: Still no one wanted it at the asking price, and debate over what to do with the property continued. *The New York Times* in 1960 reported the results of a design competition among architectural students at Cooper Union and the Pratt Institute in New York, in which some notable ideas were: an atomic research center, an interdenominational religious center, a nuclear power plant for Manhattan, a world cultural center, and a nautical museum. Other ideas were a playland (hobby and recreational center), a permanent world trade fair, a hostel for displaced persons and refugees from tyrannies (such as those who fled Hungary in 1956), quarters for retired artists, and studio space for musicians. None of these, of course, were backed by investors.

The Department of Health, Education, and Welfare (HEW) tried with the GSA to find an educational or public health function for the island. The most innovative idea along these lines was put forth in 1960 by a group called "Ellis Island for Higher Education, Inc.," composed of respected professors at Columbia, Harvard, and Princeton universities, who wanted to found a college on the island endowed by the Ford and Rockefeller foundations. This and other applications had to be rejected because they failed to meet the legal asking price.

In 1962 the Senate Subcommittee on Intergovernmental Relations to Dispose of Ellis Island was formed, headed by Senator Edmund Muskie of Maine. The subcommittee undertook to evaluate the various proposals at hand and meanwhile asked the GSA to withhold further action until the subcommittee had concluded its hearings. A growing faction, consisting of public officials and private citizens alike, felt that Ellis Island should be preserved as a monument to American immigration.

For the next year the subcommittee deliberated, during which time suggestions for use of the island continued to pour in. Among them was a design inspired by Frank Lloyd Wright, who had died three years earlier, while this project was still in the planning stages. This 8,000-resident, self-contained "dream city of the future"—named "The Key" in honor of Ellis Island's past—was submitted by Wright's son-in-law, William Wesley Peters, through a New York City development corporation. Wright had not thought any of the existing buildings worth saving, so his plan called for leveling them all and building an apartment-hotel-retail complex, "a shimmering crystal city." Although interesting conceptually, it was a purely commercial venture that had little to do with the historical importance of the island, and both the GSA and the subcommittee rejected the idea.

In September 1963 Senator Muskie called a meeting in Washington of all interested parties—which included the mayors of New York City and Jersey City, officials and congressional representatives of New York State and New Jersey, and representatives from the GSA, HEW, and the Department of the Interior—to see if they could arrive at a consensus about the disposal of Ellis Island. The options were: (1) simply to sell it to the highest bidder; (2) to recommend special legislation to create one of several federal projects (for example, housing for the elderly or a mental retardation center) or one of several private, nonprofit ventures (a maritime center and nautical high school, a veterans' convalescent home, or a "Boys Town" for New York).

Main building dormitory, dining room, and stairs, summer 1982

ALL, JULIAN KAISER

DEPOSIT TRAYS AND DISHES HERE
GESCHIRR HIER ABSTELLEN
METTETE VASSOI E PIATTI QUI
POLOZYC TACY I NACZYNIE TUAJ
DEJEN BANDEJAS Y PLATOS AQUI

Since no one seemed in favor of commercial development of the island and there was no consensus about any of the other proposals (none of the factions would support anyone else's ideas or had the means to implement its own), the meeting adjourned with still no firm resolution of the dilemma. Senator Muskie recommended that the National Park Service review the possibility of using the island for a national park, monument, or recreational facility in conjunction with New Jersey's proposal for a shoreline park.

The National Park Service (NPS) had already been approached with this idea, but because they were committed to a plan to create a museum of immigration in the base of the Statue of Liberty—and fund-raising for the project was already underway—the service was reluctant to take on a project that seemed in conflict. Nevertheless, they agreed to do a feasibility study, and for the next six months NPS administrators, historians, architects, and designers surveyed Ellis Island, conducted field studies, compiled reports, and met among themselves and with various New Jersey and New York officials.

By late winter of 1963, they apparently had changed their minds. An article in *The New York Times* reported that the NPS had come to feel that the American Museum of Immigration under construction on Liberty Island, the proposed 500-acre park on the Jersey shoreline, and an additional facility at Ellis Island could complement one another. Accordingly, they submitted a report to the Senate subcommittee recommending that Ellis Island be designated a national historic site. The subcommittee decided that of all the proposals before it, this was the most worthwhile from several standpoints and advised Secretary of the Interior Morris Udall to proceed with implementing the NPS's recommendations.

A year later, on May 11, 1965, President Lyndon B. Johnson added Ellis Island to the Statue of Liberty National Monument. This put an end to any speculation about the development of the island and to any dispute over its jurisdiction. At the same time he announced the creation of a Job Corps Conservation Center in Jersey City to help with rehabilitating Ellis Island and creating Liberty State Park. A few months later the President signed into law a Congressional resolution to appropriate a maximum of $6 million for the development of Ellis Island as part of the monument. Also that year a new immigration bill was passed, doing away with the old quota system and replacing it with a law based on the skills of the applicants.

Meanwhile, the NPS had taken over the administration of Ellis Island. Some time before, the GSA, discouraged with the costs of upkeep, had turned off the power on the island and reduced the staff to one night watchman. The result was an immediate intensification of the effects of weathering and vandalism. The buildings were in a state of ruin. Thomas Pitkin, author of *Keepers of the Gate* (New York: New York University Press, 1975), visited Ellis Island that summer and wrote:

> The lack of heat in the damp atmosphere of the bay soon showed its effect in falling plaster and tiles. Leaky roofs went unrepaired. Pigeons swarmed in through broken windows, and piles of manure built up here and there in the upper stories. On the lower floors, water accumulated in places to a depth of several inches. Vegetation ran wild in the open spaces. The heavy concrete and granite seawall surrounding the island was cracking.

While doing its field studies the previous fall, the NPS had discovered that the Edward Laning mural

FRED FREEMAN, AMERICAN WEEKLY. COURTESY OF TALIESIN ASSOCIATES, SCOTTSDALE, AZ painted in the dining room in the late thirties was badly deteriorated and moved a portion of it to Liberty Island for restoration and safekeeping (several years later other portions of the mural were similarly rescued). The thought then was to eventually install it in the American Museum of Immigration. Now NPS officials are considering returning it to Ellis. In the meantime it is displayed in a room used for naturalization proceedings in a Brooklyn courthouse.

Shortly after Ellis Island became part of Liberty National Monument, Secretary Udall assigned the task of developing a restoration plan to Philip Johnson, a New York architect best known for his design of parts of Lincoln Center and the Museum of Modern Art. Johnson's idea was to use the ruined buildings themselves as part of the memorial to immigration. The main building on Island 1 and the hospital buildings on Island 2 could be stabilized for visitors to view from raised walkways. All other buildings would be demolished. The principal feature of the plan (which included a restaurant, picnic grounds, and a band shell) was a monument entitled "The Wall of 16 Million." This was a 130-foot tower, a concrete hollow cone with spiral ramps, which visitors could walk up as they read the engraved names of immigrants who had passed through Ellis Island. The monument would be situated on a treeless lawn on the vacated Island 3 and give an impressive view of the harbor, especially the Statue of Liberty. In its center would be a courtyard with a reflecting pool.

Johnson's design received mixed reviews from the NPS and architectural critics. In any case, it was far more expensive than the money allotted for it, and when archivists and statisticians at the NPS realized the difficulty of providing a bona fide list of names for the monument, the plan was discarded.

The NPS set about developing its own master plan based on the report it had done for the Senate subcommittee in 1964. The plan, approved in November 1968, divided the island into three units. The north unit, consisting of the main building and a few support structures (a maintenance facility with greenhouse for landscaping, a landing for shuttle boats, and a residence), would be essentially a formal museum area, to recall and interpret the history of immigration at Ellis Island. The south unit, on Islands 2 and 3, which would be cleared of the dangerous old hospital buildings, would be an informal recreational area with promenade, picnic grounds, restaurant, and facilities for ethnic activities such as folk dancing and craft demonstrations. The third unit, an arcade or walkway that would be a transitional area between north and south units, would include a reconstruction of the old ferry loading platform and rehabilitation of the ferry boat *Ellis Island* as an exhibit; across from it would be a reflecting pool and commemorative statuary. Total cost of the master plan was estimated at $8.7 million.

While the master plan was under consideration, the NPS made roofing and drainage repairs necessary to stabilize the buildings. Funds were virtually nonexistent, however. Because of cuts in federal spending, the $6 million designated for the rehabilitation of Ellis Island never actually materialized. When the *Ellis Island* sank at her moorings that year, beyond hiring a diving team to determine the reason, the NPS was able to do nothing to salvage the vessel. As there was no money for maintenance and security, the deterioration of the buildings from weathering, overgrowth, and vandalism continued.

In 1970 there were two peculiar attempts by minority groups to take over Ellis Island. Militant Indians from fourteen tribes, protesting the "disease, alcohol, pover-

BARBARA BENTON

Ferry slip, with the remains of the sunken Ellis Island, spring 1985

ty, and cultural desecration" wrought on Indians by the white man, attempted to land on the island from the New Jersey side. They were turned back by NPS guards; afterwards the Coast Guard established a security zone around the island and stationed two patrol boats nearby to guard against trespassers. Next, a black organization from New York City—the National Economic Growth and Reconstruction Organization, Inc. (NEGRO)—despite Coast Guard restrictions, squatted on the island and started a packaging opera-

tion. Eventually, they were granted a permit to occupy the south end of the island (presumably because they had the ways and means of contributing to the rehabilitation of Ellis Island and opening it to visitors), but by 1971 they had abandoned their project and the island.

During the administration of Richard Nixon there was a brief reconsideration of the disposal of Ellis Island. In addition to the full implementation of the NPS master plan (then re-estimated to cost close to $40 million), there were several suggestions for various

RESTORATION   175

private or joint federal-private ventures. Because of the prohibitive rehabilitation costs, Secretary of the Interior Rogers Morton suggested complete divestiture of the island. As in previous debates, none of the proposals received adequate political support, so still nothing substantial was done to alter the status quo on Ellis Island.

In 1974 Dr. Peter Sammartino, Chairman of the International Committee of the New Jersey Bicentennial Commission, took a helicopter ride over the New York Bay area and noted the condition of Ellis Island. Dr. Sammartino then visited the island and, as the son of Italian immigrants who had passed through Ellis, was appalled at the extent of the deterioration. He formed the "Restore Ellis Island Committee," which in short time was influential in having government funds appropriated for the restoration and in launching a public fund-raising campaign.

Early in 1976 President Gerald Ford approved a Congressional appropriation of $1 million for the Ellis Island restoration and a $500,000 annual budget for its operation. This finally made it possible to open the island to visitors. In preparation for the opening in May 1976, the NPS had much of the debris removed from the island and made the main building safe for visitation. The old seawall was stabilized, the ferry basin was dredged and a new dock built, and utilities were reinstalled. An interpretation plan was developed, and for the first time since its closing in 1954, the island was adequately staffed: twenty-four-hour guards were put on duty and a staff of some twenty guides and maintenance people was hired.

During that first season, the summer and fall of the nation's bicentennial year, 50,000 visitors to the Statue of Liberty boarded the ferry there and took the optional one-hour tour of Ellis Island. Visitor response was grati-

fying. The story of immigration told by the NPS guides—and the ghostly quality of the buildings themselves—produced an emotional experience for most people. It was clear that Ellis Island could be as great an attraction to tourists as the Statue of Liberty.

Each year after its opening to visitors, Ellis Island gained a broader base of public support for the creation of a national monument to the immigrants. Late in 1976 Congress authorized funding for the further study of the project, and in 1979, when funds became available, the NPS began formulating a "general management plan" for the restoration, identifying the buildings to be restored to their previous state, those to be adapted for visitor use, and those that would not be useful as part of the monument.

In 1981 the Historic Preservation Amendment was passed, in which Section 111 provides that the NPS can lease out historic properties and retain revenues within the Service for maintenance of the properties. This at last made it possible for the NPS to consider plans for a monument that could be self-maintaining, rather than entirely dependent upon Congressional funding or private donations. As the buildings of the Contagious Disease Hospital did not seem otherwise useful, the NPS immediately solicited proposals for a compatible (and profitable) use for them. Fourteen offers were received, the most advantageous of which seemed to be a convention center proposed by a New York City development company. This idea was incorporated in the general management plan, formally published in 1982.

Also in 1982 President Ronald Reagan and then Secretary of the Interior James Watt announced the formation of The Statue of Liberty–Ellis Island Centennial Commission and named Lee Iacocca, chief executive officer of Chrysler Corporation, as its chairman. The